Greening the Lyre

ENVIRONMENTAL ARTS

AND HUMANITIES

SERIES

Greening the Lyre

ENVIRONMENTAL POETICS AND ETHICS

DAVID W. GILCREST

UNIVERSITY OF NEVADA PRESS
RENO & LAS VEGAS

Environmental Arts and Humanities Series
Series Editor: Scott Slovic

University of Nevada Press, Reno, Nevada 89557 USA

Manufactured in the United States of America
Design by Kaelin Chappell

Library of Congress Cataloging-in-Publication Data
Gilcrest, David W., 1962–
Greening the lyre : environmental poetics and ethics /
David W. Gilcrest
p. cm. — (Environmental arts and humanities series)
Includes bibliographical references (p.) and index.
ISBN: 978-0-87417-494-6 (hardcover : alk. paper)
ISBN: 978-0-87417-983-5 (paperback : alk. paper)
ISBN: 978-0-87417-554-7 (ebook)
1. American poetry—20th century—History and criticism.
2. Nature in literature. 3. Conservation of natural resources
in literature. 4. Environmental protection in literature.
5. Philosophy of nature in literature. 6. Environmental policy
in literature. 7. Nature conservation in literature. 8. Ecology
in literature. 9. Ethics in literature. 10. Environmental ethics.
I. Title. II. Series
PS310.N3 G55 2002
811'.540936—dc21 2001008690

The paper used in this book meets the requirements of
American National Standard for Information Sciences—
Permanence of Paper for Printed Library Materials,
ANSI/NISO Z39.48-1992 (R2002). Binding materials
were selected for strength and durability.

This book has been reproduced as a digital reprint.

To Debra, Mack, and Abbey
"I can no longer tell
where I begin and leave off."

CONTENTS

ACKNOWLEDGMENTS

I am grateful beyond words for the generosity and patience of my mentors and teachers, including Janet Desimone, Steve Masley, Robbie Thomas, Richard Hawley, Cleopatra Mathis, Patricia Goedicke, Paul Armstrong, Bill Rossi, Jim Crosswhite, and John Gage. The debt, which I struggle to repay in and out of the classroom, endures.

I would also like to thank the entire Mesaverde crew at the University of Oregon for their constancy, intellectual challenge, and goodwill, especially David Sumner, Laird Christensen, and Peter Blakemore. David Shetzline, a true artisan of pen and fly rod, has earned my respect and thanks as an exemplar in all things philosophical and anadromous.

For their unstinting humor and support, I would like to thank my colleagues in the English Department at Carroll College. Also, Joanne Hemb at the Todd Wehr Memorial Library was a great help in securing many of the texts used in this study. Thanks also to the Carroll College Faculty Development Committee for a grant that carried this project across the finish line.

I owe special thanks to the good people at the University of Nevada Press, especially Trudy McMurrin and Monica Miceli, for the unwavering faith and professional charm with which they shepherded this black sheep into the fold.

No accounting of this work is complete without acknowledging the love and fidelity of family and friends who made it possible: William Carney Blake, John Randell Smith, Leonard Devaney, Leslie Wallace, Kelly McGhehey, Virginia Meisner, Deb Lock, and Barbara Schomburg.

To my wife and fellow traveler, Debra, who has weathered the storms and celebrated the harvest, I offer my deepest gratitude and appreciation.

Finally, a deep bow in the direction of a few exceptional places responsible for shaping the course of this book and my life. These include the Rogue River, the French River and Georgian Bay, Mount Cube, Delicate Arch, Box Death Canyon, the Bitterroot, Blackfoot, and Clark Fork Rivers, Yoho Glacier, the McKenzie and Willamette Rivers, Wheeler Peak, the Steens, the Oregon Coast, Soda Mountain, the Porcupine Mountains, and Minong/Isle Royale on Lake Superior.

For permission to reprint the poems under consideration in this study I would like to acknowledge the following:

"Corsons Inlet." Copyright © 1963 by A. R. Ammons, from *The Selected Poems, Expanded Edition* by A. R. Ammons. Used by permission of W. W. Norton & Company, Inc.

"The River" by Peter Borrelli is reprinted from *Poetry from the Amicus Journal*, Tioga Publishing Co., 1988. Used by permission of the author.

"New Ecology" by Ernesto Cardenal is reprinted from *Nicaraguan New Time*, Journeyman Press, 1988. Used by permission of the author.

"Sexual Jealousy" by Carol Frost is reprinted from *Pure*, TriQuarterly Books/Northwestern University Press, 1994. Used by permission of the author.

"Birches," "In a Glass of Cider," "The Most of It," and "Two Look at Two" by Robert Frost are reprinted from *The Poetry of Robert Frost* edited by Edward Connery Lathem, Copyright © 1942, 1944, 1951, 1962 by Robert Frost, Copyright © 1970 by Lesley Frost Ballentine, © 1916, 1923, 1969 by Henry Holt and Co., LLC. Reprinted by permission of Henry Holt & Co., LLC.

"Augury" by Seamus Heaney is reprinted from *Wintering Out*, Faber and Faber, Ltd., 1972. Used by permission worldwide of Faber and Faber, Ltd. The poem is reprinted in *Opened Ground: Selected Poems, 1966–1996*, by Seamus Heaney. Copyright © 1998 by Seamus Heaney. Reprinted in the United States by permission of Farrar, Straus and Giroux, LLC.

"Naming the Animals" by Linda Hogan is reprinted from *The Book of Medicines*, Coffee House Press, 1993. Used by permission of Coffee House Press.

"Chimney Swifts" by Mark Jarman is reprinted from *Crazyhorse* (winter 1991). Used by permission of the author.

"The Snakes of September" by Stanley Kunitz is reprinted from *Next-to-Last Things: New Poems and Essays*, the Atlantic Monthly Press, 1985. Used by permission of the Darhonsoff and Verrill Literary Agency.

"Watchers" by Robert Pack is reprinted from *Fathering the Map*, University of Chicago Press, 1993. Used by permission of the author.

"Rural Reflections," copyright © 1963, 1967, and 1993 by Adrienne Rich, from *Collected Early Poems: 1950–1970* by Adrienne Rich. Used by permission of the author and W. W. Norton & Company, Inc.

"The Message of Rain" by Norman H. Russell is reprinted from *Poetry from the Amicus Journal*, Tioga Publishing Co., 1990. Used by permission of the author.

"In the Bog Behind My House" by Ira Sadoff is reprinted from *Emotional Traffic*, David Godine, 1991. Used by permission of the author.

"B.C." by William Stafford, copyright © 1962 and 1998 by the Estate of William Stafford. Reprinted from *The Way It Is: New & Selected Poems* with permission of Graywolf Press, Saint Paul, Minnesota.

"Reading Lao-Tzu Again in the New Year" by Charles Wright is reprinted from *Negative Blue*, Farrar, Straus & Giroux, 2000. Used by permission of the author.

Greening the Lyre

SOCRATES: Even the wolf, you know, Phaedrus, has a right to an advocate, as they say.

PHAEDRUS: Do you be his advocate?

It is difficult to conceive of a region uninhabited by man.

—THOREAU, "Ktaadn"

INTRODUCTION

The subject of this study is contemporary nature poetry. It should be noted, from the start, that all three of these terms are potential troublemakers. For example, the *contemporary* nature poem might simply refer to nature poetry published relatively recently. However, this kind of definition ignores the more athletic sense of contemporaneity, the idea that the poetry of a given era (here, the most "recent") reflects a generalized attitude or mood that is more or less distinctive. The idea of contemporaneity is further complicated by correspondences between the present poetic dispensation and previous ones. Such correspondences belie claims to novelty (and especially "progress").

The term *nature* and the idea of the *nature poem* are equally thorny. The nature poem is traditionally and usefully distinguished from other types of poetry by virtue of its subject: the nonhuman aspects of the world around us. The problem with this kind of definition is that it risks dividing the human from the nonhuman along the familiar fault line of culture/nature. Such a dichotomy tends to mask *human nature,* the aspect of our existence that includes our lives lived as sheerly physical and physiological entities.

The possibility of nature as a subject for poetry is entwined in the currents and crosscurrents of English literary history. From the perspective of the early twenty-first century, the evolution of Romanticism typically marks the transformation of nature from its merely scenic or ornamental role in neoclassical poetry (when it appears at all) toward something like the subject or focus of much poetic endeavor.[1] Thus we now recognize that in the years between, say, 1712 (when Pope published "The Rape of the Lock") and 1726 (when Thomson's *The Seasons* made its way into the world), the attitude of poetry toward nature changed dramatically.

What is less clear is whether the development of a Romantic sensibility and its posture toward the nonhuman actually represent as radical a shift as this thumbnail history suggests. It can be argued, for example, that nature emerges in Romantic poetry less as an autonomous subject and more as simply the arena for the Romantic poet's exploration of his or her imaginative consciousness.

Nature did not appear as a poetic subject in its own right until the human role with respect to nonhuman nature began to be attenuated. Many factors contributed to this change: the rise of physical and biological sciences and the bodies of knowledge they contributed, the development of a geological and evolutionary sense of time that served to de-emphasize the importance of human experience and human history, and the gross degradation of the natural world, accelerated by the effects of industrialization and human population growth, that demonstrated the limits of our conceptions of nature and encouraged an understanding of nonhuman nature "on its own terms."

The idea of nature as *subject* thus corresponds with the development of what may loosely be called an *environmental* perspective: the view that all beings, including humans, exist in complex relationship to their surroundings and are implicated in comprehensive physical and physiological processes. An *environmental poetry* is consequently distinguished from other types of "nature poetry" (especially Romantic nature poetry) to the extent that it reinforces and extends this perspective. In *The Environmental Imagination*, Lawrence Buell captures this distinction by articulating four criteria for the environmental text. They are:

> 1. The nonhuman environment is present not merely as a framing device but as a presence that begins to suggest that human history is implicated in natural history.
> 2. The human interest is not understood to be the only legitimate interest.
> 3. Human accountability to the environment is part of the text's ethical orientation.
> 4. Some sense of the environment as a process rather than as a constant or a given is at least implicit in the text. (7–8)

Inasmuch as contemporary nature poetry engages these positions, it assumes an environmental orientation. That is not to say, however, that all contemporary nature poems are environmental texts; rather, contemporary nature poetry consists of environmental poems as well as other types of nature poetry, including Romantic nature poetry written recently.

Perhaps it is the case that all poetry is "environmental," not necessarily in the specific sense of Buell's definition, but because every poem implies a *place*. Certainly narrative and dramatic poetry is *situated* (*situare:* to place) somewhere, whether or not the features of place (for example, an accounting of resident and accidental flora and fauna and of the relationships that obtain among them, an indication of local and regional topography, an appraisal of seasonal and meteorological conditions, and so on) are explicitly acknowledged. The same is true for lyric poetry, at least in its aspect as the "song" of personal experience. Even poetry that concerns itself exclusively with human culture (including language) must assume physical and physiological conditions that allow for cultural activities. In this sense, contemporary nature *poetry* admits all poetic genres.

I began by saying that the subject of this study is contemporary nature poetry. I should add, however, that I have approached my subject with two fundamental questions in mind:

1. To what extent does contemporary nature poetry represent a recapitulation of familiar poetics?
2. To what extent does contemporary nature poetry engage a poetics that stakes out new territory?

My reading of contemporary nature poetry suggests that if such poetry is innovative, its novelty lies in the direction of environmentalism. As a result, in attempting to answer these two questions I ultimately find myself endeavoring to answer an additional query:

3. What are the prospects for an *environmental poetry?*

This, then, is the true subject of my study, although it will only achieve a measure of definition at the conclusion rather than at the beginning of this work.

Buell's criteria for the environmental text raise several intrinsically related issues with which I will be concerned as I address the prospects for environmental poetry. The first issue is *epistemological:* what can we know of the nonhuman, and how is our knowledge constructed? The second issue is properly *aesthetic:* how can we integrate the nonhuman into human poetic discourse? Strictly speaking, these two issues taken together circumscribe *environmental poetics.* A third issue is entailed by the rhetorical stance of environmentalism itself. As Buell's criteria indicate, the environmental text is grounded in the premise that prevailing attitudes toward nature, as a function of what we think we know and how we represent that knowledge, are demonstrably deleterious to the nonhuman and have resulted in unprecedented, and catastrophic, alterations in the natural world. If environmentalism describes the project of discovering better ways of conceptualizing the nonhuman sphere and our relationship to it, and of putting those concepts into practice, it is finally an *ethical* undertaking. The environmental poem can thus be found, in theory anyway, at the confluence of the three principal tributaries of Western intellectual inquiry: epistemology, poetics, and ethics.

Recent scholarship has initiated the search for the environmental poem. Notable efforts include John Elder's *Imagining the Earth: The Poetry and the Vision of Nature* (University of Illinois Press, 1985), Terry Gifford's *Green Voices: Understanding Contemporary Nature Poetry* (Manchester University Press, 1995), and Gyorgyi Voros's recuperation of Stevens as a linguistically savvy poet of nature in *Notations of the Wild: Ecology in the Poetry of Wallace Stevens* (University of Iowa Press, 1997). Both Voros and Leonard Scigaj, in his *Sustainable Poetry: Four American Ecopoets* (University Press of Ken-tucky, 1999), take on the ostensibly "postmodern" antireferentialist bias in contemporary literary criticism and linguistic philosophy in their efforts to reconnect word and world.

My own pursuit of the environmental poem begins in chapter 1 with an examination of the influence of ecology on contemporary nature poetry. Although normative ecology provides a productive critique of homocentric values, I argue, following Wolfgang Iser, that a sheerly ecologized poetic, while fulfilling our desire for certitude under pressure of environmental crisis, fails on epistemological and ultimately aesthetic grounds.

In chapter 2 I address the environmental implications of the trope of speaking nature. I argue that the attempt to represent nonhuman entities as speaking subjects, while serving to establish a less hierarchical relationship with the nonhuman by deprivileging human linguistic ability, is appropriately viewed as a colonizing move that remains susceptible to serious epistemological and ethical critique. I then introduce Catriona Sandilands's argument that the failure of nonhuman subjectivity provides us with the opportunity to revise our notions of democracy and democratic practice. Sandilands's theory of radical democracy suggests that in order to preserve ecocentric values we need to transform the concept of democratic subjectivity. I argue, with Donna Haraway, that the idea of nonhuman subjectivity can be usefully supplanted in aesthetic and perhaps democratic discourse by the notion of *alinguistic agency*.

I continue to address more satisfactory approaches to environmental poetry in chapter 3. In this chapter I consider the rhetorical stance of the poet. I argue that an environmental ethic does not necessitate the identification of the human and the nonhuman, whether in terms of linguistic competency or along any other dimension, and may in fact require the conservation of difference. I present readings of four poems that negotiate the epistemological and ethical implications of identification and difference. I argue finally that by resisting identification with the nonhuman by embracing an antagonistic poetics, the contemporary nature poet cultivates an ethic of restraint consistent with ecocentric values.

In the final two chapters of this study I consider the influence of hermeneutical poetics on contemporary environmental poetry. In chapter 4 I argue that the pragmatic aspect of hermeneutical poetics, grounded here in Robert Frost's theory of metaphor, makes possible a poetic practice that is both aesthetically viable and epistemologically adequate. Furthermore, when exercised in the service of environmental interests, such a poetic practice reinforces essential ecocentric values, as we see in A. R. Ammons's "Corsons Inlet."

In chapter 5 I argue that the more skeptical aspect of hermeneutical poetics, represented here by Kenneth Burke's rhetorical and linguistic theories and reflected in Wallace Stevens's own strategies of metaphor, represents the most successful approach to environmental poetry. As applied by poets like Adrienne Rich and Charles Wright, a skeptical environmental poetics also suggests the need to reconceptualize the criteria by which environmental poetry is typically recognized to include poetry that calls into question our ability to represent faithfully the nonhuman within poetic discourse. Leonard Scigaj's identification of the poetry of *référence* points our way toward just such a reconceptualization.

In completing this study I have incurred many intellectual debts that can only be partially recompensed through generous acknowledgment. I owe a particular debt, however, to Kenneth Burke, whose influence may be felt throughout these pages. I have borrowed rather brazenly many of his ideas, especially those pertaining to the function and operation of language. And in an important sense, the project as a whole takes as its model Burke's notion of "logology" developed especially in *The Rhetoric of Religion*. In that study Burke engages the rhetoric of religion to explore "the nature of language itself as a motive" (vi). My own inquiry has concerned itself with the rhetoric of "nature" and the "environment." But whereas Burke explicitly (and wisely) bracketed his analysis of "words about God" by eschewing any consideration of their potential referent, the ethical dimension of environmental discourse compels an examination of the relationship between our "words about nature" and that to which they ostensibly refer. My happy conceit here is that an analysis of the rhetoric of nature also contributes to our understanding of "the nature of language itself as a motive."

Finally, my reading of contemporary nature poetry has reinforced the respect I hold toward the work of Robert Frost. Too often described as a pale modernist, or dismissed as "merely" a regional poet, Frost emerges from this study as a central figure in the evolution of hermeneutical poetics and discursive ethics. To the extent that contemporary environmental poetry is grounded in such a poetic practice, it, too, owes a debt to Frost. My hope is that a study such as this will serve to reinvigorate interest in Frost's poetry and prose in the context of ecocritical inquiry.[2]

And may we have neither the mania of the One
Nor the delirium of the Many—
But both the Union and the Diversity—

—KENNETH BURKE, "Dialectician's Hymn"

CHAPTER I

Toward a Rhetoric of Ecological Poetics

Definitions and Method

Like all titles, "Toward a Rhetoric of Ecological Poetics" functions, to use Kenneth Burke's formula, as both goal and goad.[1] To avoid unnecessary confusion at the outset, my first step will be to clarify these titular terms. I will then turn to the "ecological" poem against the background of scientific and normative ecology. My reading will pay particular attention to the hermeneutic premises that inform the production of the ecological poem. An analysis of these premises suggests that the strength of ecological hermeneutics, its profound and ambitious perspicuity, is also its greatest literary weakness. I will argue, following Wolfgang Iser, that ecological poetry, while staging the fulfillment of our desire to be and to have ourselves under pressure of ecological crisis, also forecloses ontological possibilities and sacrifices degrees of truthfulness. This foreclosure and sacrifice are most generously a pragmatic gambit, the aim of which is the preservation of the material conditions that are the prerequisites to the play of our being. Less generously, ecological poetics represent a retreat from aesthetic, epistemological, and ethical values, especially in light of an alternative poetics less concerned with compensation.

To begin with, then: *rhetoric*. The term has embodied many different meanings over a very long period of time, as even a passing familiarity with the rhetorical tradition must attest. This observation is a cliché, certainly, but one bearing some practical wisdom. Rhetoric, as an idea or amalgamation of ideas, has exhibited a truly remarkable, even profligate, ability to reflect the aspirations of those who would put it to work. The history of the idea of rhetoric thus provides both cautionary and encouraging lessons: cautionary, in that the term's elasticity proves foolish any attempt to circumscribe its significance; encouraging, in that rhetoric's longevity affirms its abiding utility.

With this double-edged sword in hand, I would like to borrow, for the purposes of the present inquiry, Aristotle's sense of rhetoric as "the faculty of perceiving the available means of persuasion." One of the more interesting aspects of this well-worn definition is that it presents rhetoric not simply as eloquence, or as, in its most degraded formulation, merely the ornamental quality of discourse, but rather as a *skill* or *talent* with the potential for empowering the rhetorician. It was the ostensible *power* of rhetoric that provoked Socrates' famous attack against the Sophists, the itinerant teachers who professed the rhetorical arts. The Sophists were in fact a diverse group, but they shared a common belief that a transcendental or universal Truth either does not exist or is hopelessly inaccessible to mere mortals.[2] Socrates complained that without knowledge of Truth, teaching a person to speak effectively was like "putting a knife in the hands of a madman in the crowd" (*Gorgias* 469c ff.). While admitting that rhetorical skill can indeed allow one to affect the beliefs of an audience irrespective of the truth of those beliefs, Aristotle defended rhetoric by arguing that skill in rhetorical analysis allows us to recognize when and how our own beliefs are being influenced. Thus Aristotle's defense of rhetoric was motivated, in part, by the need for rhetorical self-defense. He writes, "it would be strange if an inability to defend oneself by means of the body is shameful, while there is no shame in an inability to use speech." And since the use of speech "is more characteristic of humans than is use of the body," he concludes that rhetorical self-defense must be judged to be as natural as corporeal self-defense (*Rhetoric* 1355A).

From the perspective of a speaker or writer, rhetorical power is most simply the ability to connect with, and perhaps move, an audience. From the perspective of an auditor or reader, however, the power of rhetoric is the power to identify the various *pisteis* (sing. *pistis*), or means of persuasion, employed by one's interlocutor. As George Kennedy demonstrates, Aristotle himself varies his use of the term *pistis* in different contexts; his definitions include "proof, means of persuasion, belief" (30). Thomas Conley translates the term to mean "conviction" or, in the plural, "persuasives" (317, 14). In the *Rhetoric*, Aristotle distinguishes two categories of "persuasives": artistic (*entekhnikē*) and nonartistic (*atekhnikē*). Artistic persuasives are those invented by a speaker and include "the presentation of the character of the speaker as trustworthy, moving the emotions of the audience, and the use of logical argument." Nonartistic persuasives include such things as "laws, witnesses, contracts, evidence of slaves, and oaths" (Kennedy 314–315). Rhetorical analysis, then, is the practice of recognizing these diverse means of persuasion in the discourse of others and yields a description of the *pisteis* in that discourse. Such a description is properly called, in turn, a rhetoric of the discourse under examination.

From this working definition of rhetoric, and rhetorical analysis, I would like to turn to the balance of my title: *ecological poetics*. If rhetoric designates a method, and the product of a method, the phrase "ecological poetics" identifies the subject of this study: the art of the ecologician, the maker of words (*logoi*) concerning an "ecologized" nature. By referring to "the art of the ecologician," I mean to underscore an obvious yet necessary point: ecology, inasmuch as it is a concept that appears in many types of texts, is an artistic creation, the result of a poetics (*poieein:* to do or make). Consequently, I take the phrase "ecological poetics" rather literally, denoting "the making of ecology," or more specifically, "the making of the ecologized text." Such a phrase posits an identifiable class or genre of text with its own set of implicit or explicit appeals.

The specific focus of this analysis is not, to be sure, the ecological text at large, but rather a subset of this genre, the ecological poem. In this chapter I am most interested in discovering the kinds of artistic persuasives, and in particular logical and emotional appeals (traditionally, *logos* and *pathos*), found in ecological poetry. The *ethos,* or character, of the poet will be the special concern of chapter 3 ("Ethos and Environmental Ethics"). Nonartistic persuasives will be noted along the way.

Ecological Science, Normative Ecology, and Poetry

No thing is single, if it lives,
But multiple its being.

—GOETHE, "Epirrhema"

I can no longer
Tell where I begin and leave off.

—KENNETH REXROTH,
"The Heart of Herakles"

What is ecological poetry? The phrase is immediately odd, like "medical sculpture" or "astronomical weaving." The current popularity of ecological rhetoric in the domains of science, spirituality, and public policy might suggest that ecological poetry is simply synonymous with "contemporary nature poetry." The purported contemporaneity of ecological concepts is challenged, however, by a more rigorous consideration of the long history of "nature poetry."[3] Robert Bly, for example, argues convincingly for locating the roots of an ecological sensibility in the ardent attacks on Cartesian philosophy and Newtonian science by Goethe, Hölderlin, and Novalis in Germany and by Blake in England.[4]

However long the ecological tradition, the term "ecology" (or rather "oecologie") was not coined until 1866. Anna Bramwell notes that two very different factors influenced the development of "oecologie": "One was an anti-mechanistic, holistic approach to biology, deriving from the German zoologist, Ernst Haeckel. The second strand was a new approach to economics called energy economics. This focused on the problem of scarce and non-renewable resources" (4). In its original conception, Haeckel's "oecologie" was grandly envisioned to be "the study of all the environmental conditions of existence" (Worster 192). The term shares, with the word "economy," the Greek root *oikos,* referring to "the family household and its maintenance." Haeckel exploited the analogical potential of the root term to marry biological and economic metaphors, as Worster observes:

> Before the advent of modern political economy, men assumed that national economic affairs could be conceived of as merely extensions of the housekeeper's budget and larder. Likewise in *Oecologie,* Haeckel suggested that the living organisms of the earth constitute a single economic unit resembling a household or family dwelling intimately together, in conflict as well as in mutual aid. (192)

As a field of scientific inquiry, ecology (as it was spelled after the International Botanical Congress of 1893) has developed around certain principles that address, if not all, then at least some of "the environmental conditions of existence." These include most especially the principle of the "ecosystem" as the scenic dimension wherein "biotic communities" inhabit "niches" while engaging in complex "energy transformations" involving biotic and abiotic elements. These "energy transformations" entail competition for resources in the form of predation, parasitism, and cooperation, with implications for population stability or instability, species diversity or scarcity, and adaptation, evolution, and coevolution.[5]

With its appeals to the biotic and abiotic relationships that obtain within and among species, ecological science represents a significant shift in perspective. It is built on a fundamental argument with Newtonian science that defines a biological entity as an autonomous and static agent, *per genus et differentia,* rather than as a member of a particular ecosystem enmeshed in intricate energy exchanges with other members of that system. The ecological perspective insists that a species not be considered independently of the evolving environmental gestalt that produces it.

The body of knowledge that ecological scientists have created concerning the relational identities of biological entities has been exploited by many writers. Appeals to this knowledge, as noted above, are conditioned by ecological science's rhetorical positioning as an alternative to Enlightenment science. The tension of this argument is ubiquitous in ecological poetry, whether or not it is explicitly acknowledged. In Stanley Kunitz's poem "The Snakes of September," for example, the speaker's encounter with two snakes signifies something quite different from a meeting between a human subject and two "objects":

> All summer I heard them
> rustling in the shrubbery,
> outracing me from tier
> to tier in my garden,
> a whisper among the viburnums,

a signal flashed from the hedgerow,
a shadow pulsing
in the barberry thicket.
Now that the nights are chill
and the annuals spent,
I should have thought them gone,
in a torpor of blood
slipped to the nether world
before the sickle frost.
Not so. In the deceptive balm
of noon, as if defiant of the curse
that spoiled another garden,
these two appear on show
through a narrow slit
in the dense green brocade
of a north-country spruce,
dangling head-down, entwined
in a brazen love-knot.
I put out my hand and stroke
the fine, dry grit of their skins.
After all,
we are partners in this land,
co-signers of a covenant.
At my touch the wild
braid of creation
trembles.

(*Next-to-Last Things* 3)

In this poem, the speaker reaches out to "stroke / the fine, dry grit" of the snakes' skins and in the process makes contact with his "partners in this land, / co-signers of a covenant." This rhetoric of contractual association presents the snakes as autonomous agents whose legal and perhaps moral stature is at least equal to that of the speaker. The snakes are two strands of "the wild / braid of creation," a relational metaphor suggestive of the intimate intricacies of an ecologized nature. That the braid "trembles" at the speaker's touch evokes both sensual excitement (anticipated by the Edenic allusion and the "entwined" snakes' formation of a "brazen love-knot," two metaphors of intersubjectivity) as well as a certain structural sensitivity or even fragility.

As a first principle of ecological poetics, then, we can observe that the ecological poem allies itself with ecological science's complaint against atomistic and mechanistic Newtonian science. In making this appeal, the ecological poem may make use of the precise grammar of ecological science; more often than not, however, the ecological poem reflects a more general sense of ecology, as we see in "The Snakes of September." Indeed, one of the more interesting characteristics of ecological poetics is the ease with which the ecologized text migrates beyond the boundaries maintained, perhaps heroically, perhaps jealously, by most ecological scientists.[6]

The difference between a strictly scientific understanding of ecology and the ecology that appears in poetry and other kinds of texts is captured, to a certain extent, in Bramwell's distinction between scientific and normative ecology. "The science of ecology," she writes, "is one that considers energy flows within a closed system." Normative ecology, on the other hand, is "the belief that severe or drastic change within that system, or indeed, any change which can damage any species within it, or that disturbs the system, is seen as wrong." "Thus," she concludes, "ecological ideas have come to be associated with the conservation of specific patterns of energy flows" (4).

The invention, or discovery, of an ethical dimension to ecology opens the door to realms of ecological discourse that, in their most extreme manifestations, bear only a vestigial resemblance to ecological science. Normative ecology is generally represented, however, as intimately affiliated with ecological science, if not derived directly from its principles. Bramwell's use of scientific vocabulary in describing normative ecology attests to this, as does Carolyn Merchant's use of similar terms in her description of an "ecocentric" environmental ethic.[7] Merchant argues that because

> science can no longer be considered value-free as the logical positivists of the early-twentieth century had insisted, proponents of ecocentric ethics look to ecology for guidelines on how to resolve ethical dilemmas. Maintenance of the balance of nature and retention of the unity, stability, diversity, and harmony of the ecosystem are its overarching goals. Of primary importance is the survival of all living and non-living things as components of healthy ecosystems. All things in the cosmos as well as humans have moral considerability. (75)

It is generally acknowledged that normative ecology finds its genesis in Aldo Leopold's description of the Land Ethic in *A Sand County Almanac,* first published in 1949. According to Leopold, "The first ethics dealt with the relation between individuals; the Mosaic Decalogue is an example. Later accretions dealt with the relation between the individual and society; democracy to integrate social organization to the individual." He noted, however, "There is as yet no ethic dealing with man's relation to land and to the animals and plants" (238). Leopold argued further, "The extension of ethics to this third element in human environment is . . . an evolutionary possibility and an ecological necessity" (239). The sequences of this extension, he observed, "may be described in ecological as well as in philosophical terms":

> An ethic, ecologically, is a limitation on freedom of action in the struggle for existence. An ethic, philosophically, is a differentiation of social from anti-social conduct. These are two definitions of one thing. The thing has its origin in the tendency of interdependent individuals or groups to evolve modes of co-operation. The ecologist calls these symbioses. Politics and economics are advanced symbioses in which the original free-for-all competition has been replaced, in part, by co-operative mechanisms with an ethical content. (238)

"The land ethic," he concluded, "simply enlarges the boundaries of the community to include soils, waters, plants, and animals, or collectively: the land" (239).

As many critics have noted, the derivation of normative ethics from the principles of ecological science runs afoul of the "fact/value problem," distinguished by David Hume, or it commits what G. E. Moore called the "naturalistic fallacy."[8] At bottom, the fact/value problem and the naturalistic fallacy both address the putative legitimacy of grounding ethical claims in ontological assertions. Without taking a stand on this point, we can simply observe that normative ecology's appeal to ecological science is, rhetorically speaking, an appeal to the authority that science may be seen to confer. Such an appeal, if not sheerly fallacious, is at least paradoxical: what are we to make of an ethic which, as described by some ecologicians, both informs, and is a product of, ecological science?

However constituted, normative ecology contributes several important principles to an ecological poetics. We have already noted its essential rhetorical stance against Newtonian science. In addition, normative ecology commends, in Merchant's terminology, the ostensible "unity, stability, diversity, and harmony" of natural systems, values that are subsumed under the rubric "interconnectedness and reciprocity" (11). Furthermore, this ethic entails, in its most ecocentric formulations, a radical egalitarianism that refuses to privilege human interests over the interests of nonhuman species.

Crisis, Revolution, and Ecological Poetics

As a way to tease out some additional principles of ecological poetics, I would like to turn next to a poem written by Ernesto Cardenal, a priest and poet who became minister of culture in the FSLN government of Nicaragua. The poem, "New Ecology," will be useful to our discussion because it foregrounds two crucial properties of the ecologized text: crisis and revolution.

The poem begins with images of nature rejuvenated. "New Ecology" is not a mere paean to burgeoning Nicaraguan fauna, however. The poem quickly sets its sights on the environmental degradation perpetrated by the Somoza dictatorship:

> In September more coyotes were seen
> round San Ubaldo.
> More alligators shortly after the triumph,
> in the rivers near San Ubaldo.
> More rabbits in the road and grisons . . .
>
> The bird population has tripled, they say,
> especially the tree duck.
> The noisy ducks fly down to swim
> where they see the water shining.
>
> Somoza's men also destroyed
> lakes, rivers and mountains.
> They diverted rivers for their estates.
> The Ochomogo dried up last summer.
> The Sinecapa dried
> because of the great landowners' tree-felling.
>
> The Matagalpa Rio Grande ran dry during the war,
> over the plains of Sebaco.
> They built two dams on the Ochomogo
> and capitalist chemical waste
> crashed into the river
> whose fish staggered like drunks.
>
> The River Boaco has filthy water.
> The Moyuá lagoon dried up. A Somoza colonel
> stole the lands from the peasants and built a dam.
> The Moyuá lagoon for centuries so lovely where it lay.
> (But now the little fishes will come back.)
> They felled and dammed.

Few iguanas in the sun, few armadillos.
Somoza sold the green Caribbean turtle.
They exported sea turtle and iguana eggs in lorries.
The caguama turtle is becoming extinct.

José Somoza has been putting an end
to the sawfish in the Great Lake.
Extinction threatens the ocelot
with its soft wood-coloured pelt,
and the puma and the tapir in the mountains
(like the peasants in the mountains).

And poor River Chiquito! Its disgrace
shames the whole country.
Somoza's ways befouling its waters.
The River Chiquito of León, choked with sewage,
and effluent from soap and tanning factories,
white waste from soap, red from tanneries,
its bed bestrewn with plastic junk,
chamber pots and rusty iron.
That was Somoza's legacy.
(We must see it running clear and sweet again
singing its way to the sea.)

All Managua's filthy water in Lake Managua
and chemical waste.
And over in Solentiname,
on the isle of La Zanata a big white heap
of stinking sawfish bones.

But now the sawfish and the freshwater shark
can breathe again.
Once more Tisma's waters mirror many herons.
It has lots of little grackles,
garganeys, tree ducks, kiskadees.

And flowers are flourishing.
Armadillos are very happy with this government.
We are recovering forests, streams, lagoons.
We are going to decontaminate Lake Managua.

Not only humans longed for liberation.
All ecology groaned. The revolution
is also for animals, rivers, lakes and trees.

(*Nicaraguan New Time* 60–62)

Cardenal describes rivers dammed and dried up, Lake Managua choked with industrial chemicals, and animals like the caguama turtle, the sawfish, and the ocelot threatened with extinction. As a catalog of ecological devastation, "New Ecology" becomes an unrelenting indictment of Somoza and the capitalists whose combined rapacity ravaged Nicaragua's once magnificent natural environment.

"New Ecology" ends where it begins, with nature in recovery, balance restored: "But now the sawfish and the freshwater shark / can breathe again. / Once more Tisma's waters mirror many herons. / It has lots of little grackles, / garganeys, tree ducks, kiskadees." The change in nature's disposition reflects, of course, the revolutionary political changes in Nicaragua. Cardenal credits the new regime with the renaissance of nature in his homeland. For Cardenal, the fate of the Nicaraguan people cannot be divorced from the fate of the land and its nonhuman inhabitants: "Not only humans longed for liberation. / All ecology groaned. The revolution / is also for animals, rivers, lakes, and trees." Humans are not the sole beneficiaries of the government's revolutionary policies. According to the poem, nonhuman nature is served by, and clearly approves of, the new political dispensation: "Armadillos are very happy with this government."

"New Ecology" is prototypical of ecological poetry in that it finds its origin in, and is a response to, ecological crisis. No other attribute better distinguishes ecological poetry than its presumption of environmental fragility and looming disintegration. Ecological poets are thus preeminently "immodest" in the sense Robert Frost gives the term. "[Y]ou will often hear it said," observed Frost, "that the age of the world we live in is particularly bad. I am impatient of such talk. . . . It is immodest of a man to think of himself as going down before the worst forces ever mobilized by God" (Rotella 62). Ecological poets are easily more patient of such talk than Frost; by and large they do believe that the globe is in an unprecedented mess, though they are more likely to see the forces of destruction as "mobilized" by their own species rather than by God.

As it depicts the ecological crisis that gripped Somoza's Nicaragua, "New Ecology" also invokes the quintessentially Romantic idea that some kind of revolution is necessary to effectively redress the problem. Something dramatic, something radical, must be done to liberate the groaning biomasses. That the ideas of crisis and revolution are yoked in ecological poetry is hardly surprising; as a rhetorical strategy, crisis creates the opportunity for revolutionary change.[9] Crisis also admits the possibility of despair, of course, and ecological crisis the possibility of ecological despair. But even the jeremiad, whether in its spiritual or ecological form, is not sheerly despairing. The jeremiad is necessarily *prospective* in that its lamentation is aimed at rectifying unsatisfactory conditions; the poetry of true despair is, in principle, a contradiction in terms, as the rhetorical (that is, suasive) aspect of poetry belies the hopelessness of real despair. The poetry of true despair is simply never written. "New Ecology" is perhaps unusual only in that it presents a revolutionary fait accompli. Cardenal's unmitigated enthusiasm for the remedies authorized by the Sandinista revolt reflects his partisan brio, the optimism of the newly victorious revolutionary. Formally considered, the sense of utopian satisfaction ultimately communicated in "New Ecology" is but the perfection of the idea of revolution made possible by the idea of crisis. "New Ecology" thus provides a model for the revolutionary ambitions of a poetry whose reason for being is to move us from crisis and instability to harmonious balance.

While crisis and revolution in "New Ecology" are presented in explicitly political terms (the land is healing now that responsible humans are in charge), the revolutionary character of ecology is not essentially political, at least as politics is traditionally construed. Politics can be more than the brute distribution of power, and political revolution may serve ecological poets like Cardenal as a kind of shorthand for a complex set of ethical, psychological, and spiritual transformations. These transformations may be presented as a novel development in human affairs or, alternatively, as a recuperation of a golden age of balance and harmony. Many ecologicians want it both ways. For example, Merchant argues that the ecological revolution

> represents as profound a transformation as the one which occurred during the scientific revolution of the seventeenth century. It would be so fundamental that it would entail new metaphysical, epistemological, religious, psychological, sociopolitical, and ethical principles. (85)

On the other hand, the "postmodern" sensibility of the ecological revolution represents, says Merchant, the recovery of Renaissance organicism and the concomitant reanimation of a nature rendered inanimate by the Enlightenment's "mechanistic framework of domination" (11). Similarly, David Ray Griffin maintains that the ecological crisis stems from the "disenchantment," at the hands of modern science, philosophy, theology, and art, of a once "enchanted" world. This "disenchantment" demands, according to Griffin, the transformation, or "reenchantment," of our attitude toward the nonhuman (2). But like Merchant, Griffin contends that this "postmodern organicism" entails nothing short of "a new science, a new spirituality, and a new society" (30, xiii). Max Oelschlaeger's historical perspective is somewhat wider, though the form is the same. He tracks the fall of human culture from an organic, Paleolithic culture into Neolithic civilization severed from its natural roots. For Oelschlaeger, the ecological revolution serves as a recovery of the organic Paleolithic worldview in the name of what he terms "posthistoric primitivism" (*Idea* 12).[10]

Most ecologicians would agree that revolutionary changes in

human culture are predicated on a revolution in human psychology. "If, as environmental philosophers contend, western metaphysics and ethics need revision before we can address today's environmental problems," writes Lawrence Buell, summarizing this perspective, "then the environmental crisis involves a crisis of the imagination the amelioration of which depends on finding better ways of imaging nature and humanity's relation to it" (2). This outline of ecological poetics serves to reflect the different kinds of appeals that together encompass the broad strategies ecologicians have employed as they attempt to articulate "better ways of imaging nature and humanity's relation to it." These include, in sum: (1) a critique of "nonorganic" (i.e., atomistic, mechanistic) conceptual schemas and the cultural institutions based on them; (2) the identification of environmental crisis, seen as the product of these "nonorganic" conceptual schemas; (3) an appeal to revolutionary transformations in psychology, ethics, religion, and politics; (4) an appeal to ecological science to authorize ethical claims of revolutionary transformation; and (5) the derivation of an ecocentric ethic of interconnectedness, reciprocity, and, in some instances, radical egalitarianism.

Ecological Poetics in "Watchers"

The rhetoric of scientific and normative ecology has had a tremendous influence on the production of nature poetry, particularly in the past thirty years. One poem that exemplifies this influence is Robert Pack's "Watchers":

> Photographed from the moon, [the Earth] seems to be a kind of organism. It is plainly in the process of developing, like an enormous embryo. It is, for all its stupendous size and the numberless units of its life forms, coherent. Every tissue is linked for its viability to every other tissue.
>
> —LEWIS THOMAS, *The Medusa and the Snail*

And so I'm linked to you
like cells within a growing embryo,
and you are linked to me,
and we, together, linked to everyone
as watchers from the moon can see.

The patient watchers from the moon can tell
what currents pushing through the tide
direct vast spawnings from the swaying deep,
and what ancestral pathways
through the buoyant air wedged wild geese keep

inscribed within their brains
that safely store stupendous images—
range after range of mountain snow,
and shadowed woodland green,
blue sky reflected in blue sea below.

Although they see all parts as one,
wholly dependent and yet numberless,
the watchers from the moon
surmise some flaw may be developing,
some rampant cells may soon

outgrow the rest, as if they knew their lives
were all life meant. And yet, at least
for now, the watchers from the moon are full
of admiration, awe,
each tissue seems connected, viable—

like you and me, together,
linked as one with our increasing kind,
taking dominion everywhere,
now cultivating forests, now the seas,
now blasting even through the air.

The membrane of the sky
holds in accumulated oxygen,
welcomes the visible, good light,

protects from lethal ultraviolet,
and guards against the flight

of random meteors that burn out,
harmless at the edge of our home space, as if
by miracle, although
just friction from our atmosphere is what
the watchers from the moon must know

keeps us alive and linked
each to the other, each to the sunlit cycles
of exhaling plants and trees.
For pollination, fruits and flowers have
warm winds and their obliging bees;

forests renew themselves from their decay,
aided by intermittent rain;
and plankton, drifting in the sun to breed,
provide the herring and the whale
with all the food they need

to keep revolving life alive
in this appointed place—
to which we're linked and which replenishes
ambrosia of the air
and animates the sea that says

Coherence is the law
we must obey, although the watchers see
certain relentless cells below,
dividing, and divided from the rest,
forming a monster embryo.
Like cells within a growing embryo.

(*Fathering the Map* 264)

In this poem, the observers on the moon provide a point of view that encompasses the totality of terrestrial life. "Watchers" is thus the poetic analog of the image, taken by Apollo astronauts, of the earth floating in space, a photograph that likely served, in addition to the passage from *The Medusa and the Snail*, as the inspiration for the poem. From their removed and timeless perspective, the exceedingly "patient" lunar observers are able to perceive the drama of life on earth. They regard terrestrial creatures not as static and isolated entities but as dynamic manifestations of life able to negotiate "currents" and "ancestral pathways" according to the instinctual wisdom "inscribed within their brains." These watchers are thus consummate ecologists, attending to, among other things, the abiotic prerequisites of life: "The membrane of the sky" that filters out "lethal ultraviolet," incinerates "random meteors," and "keeps us alive and linked / each to the other, each to the sunlit cycles / of exhaling plants and trees." Moreover, the watchers understand the essentially interdependent nature of life on our planet, the mutually beneficial business transacted between "fruits and flowers" and "obliging bees," the complex energy transformations that occur as "forests renew themselves from their decay," and the intricacies of the protein chain that links plankton and herring and whale, thus keeping "revolving life alive / in this appointed place."

And though the watchers maintain the ultimate view of earth's ecological unity ("they see all parts as one, / wholly dependent and yet numberless"), they notice as well the potential threat posed by the "growing embryo" of humanity. While the embryo's "cells" are assuredly interconnected ("we, together, linked to everyone"), certain perturbations in the embryo suggest, under lunar scrutiny, that "some flaw may be developing." With obstetrical authority, the watchers diagnose possible fetal cancer: "some rampant cells may soon / outgrow the rest." Significantly, the cancer is caused by, to use David Ehrenfeld's phrase, the arrogance of humanism: for these rogue human cells presume "their lives / were all life meant." The poem underscores this vanity by twice mentioning interconnection *within* the human species, once at the beginning of the poem, as a kind of postulate or unearned conclusion, and once in the middle of the poem, a repetition that might suggest a nervous *uncertainty* as to human interconnection, suggestive as well of a symptomatic obsession with intraspecies affiliation. The point is driven home at the end of the poem when "certain relentless cells" are described as "divided from the rest, / forming a monster embryo."

Nowhere in "Watchers" do we see humanity in productive association with nonhuman species. When the watchers pull back from their concern over the "rampant cells," their admiration is attenuated, "each tissue" only "*seems* connected, viable" (emphasis added). Moreover, this diluted optimism is immediately undercut in the subsequent stanza. In an ironic echo of Stevens's "Anecdote of the Jar," the watchers observe the human race "taking dominion everywhere / now cultivating forests, now the seas, / now blasting even through the air." While the metaphor of cultivation might appear ethically neutral, the effect is only momentary, blasted by the image of people "blasting even through the air." The rhetoric of domination cuts through any ostensibly comforting rhetoric of human stewardship.

The watchers provide a thoroughly ecologized epistemological and ethical viewpoint. Their observations are structured around principles of ecological science and ethics. The poem even concludes with an ecological moral that serves both as lesson and warning: "*Coherence is the law / we must obey.*" Interestingly enough, this edict is not pronounced by the watchers but rather by the sea, as if to suggest that ecological wisdom comes from the earth itself, though it may be gleaned by those who watch patiently and listen carefully. The poem stops short of offering a revolutionary program to combat the growing human threat, which becomes, by the end of the poem, an actuality: "the watchers see / certain relentless cells below, / dividing, and divided from the rest, / forming a monster embryo." This is the poem's other warning, that the balance of creation (including the lunarians?) might have to take up torches and pitchforks and march on the castle of humanity to confront the monster.

But that isn't quite right. The rhetoric of "Watchers" invokes not the (Hollywoodized) Frankenstein or Dracula myths but rather the logic of abortion to take care of the earth's most selfish of genes.

I have chosen to focus on "Watchers" at some length to illustrate how the principles of ecology can inform the contemporary poet's attitude toward the natural world and humanity's relationship to it. By drawing on the rhetorical appeals that characterize scientific and especially normative ecology, "Watchers" represents a large class of contemporary nature poems, one that is often equated with contemporary nature poetry itself. But while the influence of ecology is certainly pervasive in contemporary nature poetry, not all contemporary nature poems are so thoroughly ecologized as is "Watchers." One reason contemporary nature poetry is not in fact synonymous with ecological poetry is due to the lingering influence of Romantic sensibilities (which lay claim to Nature almost as a matter of divine right). A second reason stems from the implications of the hermeneutical precepts that underlie ecological poetics, as we shall see in the next section.

Conditions of Knowledge and Representation

With a working definition of ecological poetics now in hand, we can begin to discern the epistemological premises that inform them. Two questions will bear on our analysis: (1) What is the perceived status of ecological knowledge? (2) What are the aesthetic implications of a poetics grounded in such knowledge?

In his account of the history of ecology, Worster reflects on the evolution of the term:

> At first nothing more than an unusual coupling of Greek roots, it eventually assumed a complicated burden of meaning that was a

> good deal more flexible and inclusive, perhaps, than its author anticipated. It became in its own right a potent cultural presence. (191)

There are those, of course, who begrudge this inclusivity, seeing in the appropriation of ecology an ill-fated degradation of the term's ostensible scientific purity. In their *Principles of Ecology*, for instance, R. J. Putman and S. D. Wratten decry the nonscientific or quasi-scientific use of the term:

> More debasedly, the word 'Ecology' is used politically, and usually uninformedly, as an easy analogue for the environment and its natural function or as an abbreviation for 'Human ecology': a sense in which we shall endeavour to avoid using it in this volume. (13)

Further, Putman and Wratten announce that they "have deliberately avoided a descriptive, 'habitat' or taxonomic approach to the material, feeling that Ecology must be shown to be a quantitative, exact science, with certain underlying principles and laws as fundamental as the laws of pure physics" (11). One can only imagine what these authors think of even more "inexact" uses of ecology.[11]

While efforts to maintain the conceptual purity of ecology are entered into with obvious determination, the conspicuous fact about ecological discourse is its tenacious proliferation into realms unimagined and unendorsed by many, if not most, ecological scientists. And just as ecology cannot be confined within the pale of science, neither can it be restricted to any particular social, economic, or spiritual articulation. Merchant underscores this point by noting:

> Although radical ecology pushes for change and social transformation, it is not a monolithic movement. It has many schools of thought and many action groups. Its branches are often at odds in goals and values, as well as techniques and specifications. These produce conflicts and heated debates within the larger movement resulting in a variety of approaches to resolving environmental problems. (13)

While Merchant is quite right to acknowledge the real diversity of ecological discourse, I would like to argue that a relatively constant feature of ecological discourse as a whole is what might be called its "hermeneutic self-confidence." This self-confidence may ultimately be traced to the authority vested in the ontological descriptions offered by ecological science; in general, though, it derives from the more ubiquitous sense that we have finally discovered the truth of our being, and the being of others, in ecological, relational identifications. The ecologician remains eminently sanguine about his or her ability to ascertain the ontological conditions of nature, to diagnose correctly the causes of environmental crisis, and to prescribe faithfully a revolutionary program that would deliver the globe from environmental disaster. It is this confidence that Gary Snyder exudes at the end of his ecological manifesto, "For All":

> I pledge allegiance to the soil
> of Turtle Island,
> one ecosystem
> in diversity
> under the sun
> With joyful interpenetration for all.
>
> (*Axe Handles* 113–114)

In pledging "allegiance to the soil / of Turtle Island" (that is, the North American continent, according to some Native American tribes), Snyder also professes his faith in the principles of ecology, which he regards as a real and abiding knowledge of place. It is a knowledge that deserves allegiance and affords, as Snyder sees it, not just a relatively neutral ontology of "interconnectedness and reciprocity" but rather an ontology of "joyful interpenetration" worth celebrating in a poem.

Snyder's enthusiasm may be fetching, but it also glosses over significant problems raised by the epistemological orientation of ecological discourse. Worster perceptively recognizes in this epistemological orientation "the ultimate paradox of the Age of Ecology":

> As the world around us grows ever more complex, causing our responses to appear partial, relative, situational, or archaic, we turn more and more to science for leadership. Here at last, we have been told—and want to believe—is a sure thing. Thus we have almost all become converts to the positivist creed. It is not the first time in history that men have listened intently to the power they most feared.
>
> The ecologist is the most recent of science's prophets. He offers not only a credible explanation for the way nature works, but also something of a metaphysical insight, a set of ethical precepts—perhaps even a revolutionary program. (343–344)

I would only add that this paradox is not confined to the enterprise of ecological science but in fact confronts all those who approach nature from the same direction as the ecological scientist, including, and perhaps especially, the poet.

The hermeneutic self-confidence that marks the reach of ecological discourse qualifies that discourse as, to use Wolfgang Iser's terminology, a "global conceptualization." According to Iser, a "global conceptualization" is fundamentally an "explanation of origins" that presents "what in life appeared to have been sealed off from access" ("Representation" 244–245). In this light, ecological discourse makes accessible our origins as interconnected and reciprocal beings. Ecological discourse thus "stages" the attainment of what has been hidden. "The need for such a staging," says Iser, "arises out of man's decentered position: we are, but do not have ourselves. Wanting to have what we are, that is, to step out of ourselves in order to grasp our own identity, would entail having final assurances as to our origins, but as these underlie what we are, we cannot 'have' them" (244).

Insofar as ecological discourse represents a final assurance as to our origins, it remains an attempt to present what is ultimately inaccessible. That is not to say that ecological discourse is therefore pathetic or naive; rather, it is a characteristic response to the basic human need to "grasp our own identity" so that we might know what it is to be human. Iser notes that our reluctance to accept the disjunction between being and having ourselves

> is evinced by the multiplicity of our attempts to conceptualize life. Anthropologically speaking, these conceptualizations are motivated by our inherent drive to make accessible the inaccessible, and this holds true even of the pragmatic solutions offered by our many ideologies, which in the final analysis are meant to determine what eludes our grasp. It is therefore little wonder that one set of concepts is frequently rejected and subsequently replaced by another, which in turn has to be exposed as a fiction merely designed to compensate for what has been withheld from us. Whatever shape or form these various conceptualizations may have, their common denominator is the attempt to explain origins. (244–245)

Iser suggests that there are two fundamentally different literary strategies available for responding to our desire to make accessible the inaccessible, strategies that entail distinct aesthetic and epistemological effects. He notes that literature "can fulfill the desire by providing an image of having the unavailable, or it can stage the desire itself, and so raise the question of the origin and nature of that desire—though the question, of course, is unanswerable" (247). Literature that is aimed at explanation in fact sacrifices the essential "fictionalizing" aspect of literature. In the process, such quasi-literature risks its own obsolescence as it forecloses ontological potential. By staging the fulfillment of our desire to have ourselves, "literature will come close to what conceptualizations of life intend to achieve, and consequently historical necessities will condition the form of this desired fulfillment" (247). As a result, Iser warns, "The greater the emphasis on compensation, the more dated will the solution appear to future generations of readers" (247). Compensatory literature also sacrifices degrees of truthfulness in that the satisfaction of our desire with a "global conceptualization" preempts the play of alternative ontologies. According to Iser, "Play . . . is something that the global conceptualizations of life cannot afford to incorporate into their explanatory patterns; they have to be one-dimensional in view of the finality of the explanation to be achieved and the certainties to be provided by them" (245).

Iser acknowledges, "Of course literature also springs from the same anthropological need, since it stages what is inaccessible, thus compensating for the impossibility of knowing what it is to be. But literature is not an explanation of origins," he maintains, "it is a staging of the constant deferment of explanation, which makes the origin explode into its multifariousness" (244–245). Moreover, ecological poetry, conditioned by the particular historical necessities that give rise to the form of our desire (most immediately, the sense of environmental crisis), risks its own relevance by sacrificing literary value on the altar of certitude. The literary merit of such poetry, and its ability to address the "multifariousness" of being, may be said to be inversely proportional to the magnitude of its explanatory ambition.

In his poem "Augury," Seamus Heaney dramatizes the psychological effects created by the environmental crisis. In the process he also enacts the aesthetic predicament that confronts environmentally minded poets. The poem begins with a disturbing portrait of despoiled nature:

> The fish faced into the current,
> Its mouth agape,
> Its whole head opened like a valve.
> You said 'It's diseased.'
>
> A pale crusted sore
> Turned like a coin

And wound to the bottom,
Unsettling silt off a weed.

The poem then turns to consider our response to this kind of environmental degradation:

We hang charmed
On the trembling catwalk:
What can fend us now
Can soothe the hurt eye

Of the sun,
Unpoison great lakes,
Turn back
The rat on the road.

(*Wintering Out* 53)

The catwalk trembles, threatening to dash us to pieces. "We hang charmed"—a curious phrase, combining a mode of death (both execution and suicide) with the sense of paralysis. But are we charmed as the deer is charmed by the onrushing headlights? Or is Heaney professing a muted optimism in our native abilities, our "charms," to survive?

The following lines fail to resolve these ambiguities. They read like an assertion ("What can fend us now / *Can* soothe . . . [emphasis added]"), but the line break forces the question ("What can fend us now"?). And the verb is a little odd, at least to American ears: *fend:* to defend, to ward off, turn aside, keep out or at a distance, to make an effort, to argue, to wrangle. What can defend us, the poem seems to ask, what can clean things up, turn back the rat of our toxic nightmare?

The rat on the road compels a response. But as "Augury" illustrates, the nature of that response is far from obvious, hidden somewhere between fear and hope. While the discourses of ecology have provided some hope as we begin to face up to our environmental responsibilities, poetry's role in turning back the rat cannot be confined to ecological exegesis. Iser's anthropological criticism raises the possibility of an environmental poetics that stages our need to respond to the rat in the road rather than offering us an ecological charm to turn it away. But can we afford the luxury of such a poetry?

Given the apparent urgency of environmental crisis, it is reasonable to ask whether we will be better off with a poetry that helps us understand our need for an explanation of our origins instead of poetry that explains our origins in such a way that we can approach the rat with self-confidence. With enough faith in ecology, we might easily settle for the latter, which, while sacrificing aesthetic and epistemological values, offers a chance to preserve the material conditions that permit the play of being (including the play we call poetry).

A survey of environmental poetry extending beyond the ecological reveals a number of poets who are unwilling to make the aesthetic and epistemological sacrifices required by a sheerly ecologized poetics. Instead, these poets explore the way our desire for meaning shapes how we understand ourselves and our place in the environment. Just how such a poetry can serve as a relevant, and ethical, response to environmental crisis, just how it can "Turn back / the rat on the road" while conserving aesthetic and epistemological (and political) values, is the subject of the remaining chapters.

Thus may we help Thine objects
To say their say—
Not suppressing by dictatorial lie,
Not giving false reports
That misrepresent their saying.

—KENNETH BURKE, "Dialectician's Hymn"

CHAPTER 2

Green Speech: The Trope of Speaking Nature

Ecocentrism, Democracy, and the Voice of Nature

B.C.

The seed that met water spoke a little name.

(Great sunflowers were lording the air that day;
this was before Jesus, before Rome; that other air
was readying our hundreds of years to say things
that rain has beat down on over broken stones
and heaped behind us in many slag lands.)

Quiet in the earth a drop of water came,
and the little seed spoke: "Sequoia is my name."

(*Stories That Could Be True* 76)

To the contemporary reader, the idea of a talking seed may seem a quaint, perhaps charming aspect of this diminutive poem by William Stafford. As an example of "speaking nature," the voice of Stafford's "little seed" is but one in the great chorus of nonhuman voices to be found in poetry. The trope of speaking nature, as I shall refer to it, is in fact rather ubiquitous; it has been exploited by English-language writers at least since "the best of trees began to speak words" in the *Dream of the Rood* (c. 800 C.E.).

With the advent of ecology and an "ecologized" literary sensibility, however, the voice of nonhuman nature has taken on a significance that transcends the poetic conceit of the pathetic fallacy. This is particularly true when we consider the development of an ecocentric environmental ethic that holds that all of nature, including humans, is essentially centerless and nonhierarchical, a web of interdependent and interanimating entities. The radical egalitarianism of ecocentrism, especially in its most liberal formulations, refuses to privilege humanity on any grounds including on the basis of linguistic ability.

As Christopher Manes has noted, the rhetoric of humanism has tended to silence the voice of nature.[1] Inasmuch as humanistic philosophies distinguish humanity from nonhuman species on the basis of linguistic ability, typically equating language use with the prestige of rationality, the trope of speaking nature is employed to critique the preeminent status of Lord Man.

Differentiating, and ultimately elevating, humans on the basis of linguistic ability is foregrounded in the so-called Protagoras Myth, which has been invoked, as Stanley Fish observes, "in every defense of humanism and belles lettres" (481). The myth is an account of the purportedly consubstantial genesis of language and civilization. According to the Platonic version of this myth, Prometheus and Epimetheus are charged with distributing to all of creation the qualities proper to each species. Due to Epimetheus's poor planning, all species are suitably equipped except for man, who is left "naked and shoeless, and had neither bed nor arms of defense." Acting on humanity's behalf, Prometheus schemes to enter Olympus to steal the technical knowledge of Athene and Hephaestus, knowledge with which "man was well supplied with the means of life" (*Protagoras* 19, 20).

Thus equipped, the human species, with "cunning device," is able to "frame articulate speech and names," as well as to procure "houses to dwell in, and raiment and shoes to put on, and beds for rest, and food from the fruits of the earth" (Stewart 217). But as their arts and crafts "were only sufficient to provide them with the means of life," early humans were unable to wage war against the wild beasts who continually decimated their ranks. And though they soon began to gather themselves into cities for self-protection, they had no art of government and thus "dealt unjustly with one another, and were again in process of dispersion and destruction" (*Protagoras* 20). Zeus, fearing that the entire race might be exterminated, deigns to give humanity, in the twin gifts of "modesty" and "justice," the art of government by virtue of which men might live peaceably with one another. And as the art of war is, in the classical schema, a feature of the art of government, Zeus's gifts also afford humanity the means to wage effective war against the misanthropic wild beasts.

As James Crosswhite has noted, the Protagoras Myth is relevant to a discussion of language and nature as it serves to distinguish between "dumb" creation and the linguistically cultured species, *Homo sapiens.* Here, language (as the prerequisite for culture) is antithetical to nonhuman nature, and in fact facilitates the destruction of the nonhuman.

In the context of ecocentrism, the voice of nature contributes toward a redefinition of human/nonhuman relationships, a realignment that Gary Snyder terms "posthumanism." "The 'post' in the term *posthumanism,*" he notes, "is on account of the word *human,*" adding, "The dialogue to open next would be among all beings, toward a rhetoric of ecological relationships" (*Practice* 68).

Such a dialogue is premised on the recognition of nonhuman entities as potential interlocutors in some fashion. The contention, as Patrick Murphy observes, is that "Nonhuman others can be constituted as speaking subjects rather than merely objects of our speaking" (50). According to Murphy, constituting nonhuman others as speaking subjects is distinguished from the Romantic use of the trope of speaking nature, the effect of which is to "render nature an object for the self-constitution of the poet as speaking subject." Instead, under the sign of ecocentrism, the poet presents nature "as a character within texts with its own existence" and its own voice (49).

The move to recognize the voice of nature goes well beyond the desire for converse with the nonhuman, however, toward more explicitly political considerations. As Snyder and others have argued, the recognition of the voice of nature allows nonhuman entities to gain admittance into democratic practices in resistance to their oppression. Snyder is perhaps most sanguine about the possibility of integrating the nonhuman into democratic discourse. He calls for "a new definition of humanism and a new definition of democracy that would include the nonhuman, that would have representation from those spheres" (*Turtle Island* 106).[2] Snyder recommends as a model the "ultimate democracy" practiced in Pueblo societies, the "Kiva of Elders" within which "Plants and animals are also people, and, through certain rituals and dances given a place and a voice in the political discussions of the humans" (104). Without such representation, Snyder warns, nonhuman entities inevitably disclose the real locus of power: "If we don't do it, they will revolt against us. They will submit non-negotiable demands about our stay on the earth. We are beginning to get non-negotiable demands right now from the air, the water, the soil" (108).

In keeping with Snyder's proposition, John Seed has conceived of the "Council of All Beings," a gathering in which the nonhuman is given voice in dialogic exuberance:

> The next day, 13 of us masked creatures gathered in a circle. We put two humans in the center and then aired our grievances against this shortsighted and inconsiderate species. The first, Mountain Lion, circled the humans on all fours, growling, reprimanding, screaming and crying with grief. We each, in turn, talked about ourselves and expressed fear, bewilderment and anger toward the humans. (Stone 61–62)

However we gauge the facility of integrating nonhuman entities into democratic practices through constructs like the Kiva of Elders and the Council of All Beings, recognizing the nonhuman subject does have certain inherent advantages. It is arguably more difficult to exterminate fellow subjects than it is to eliminate mere objects (human history notwithstanding).[3] A rhetoric that emphasizes the subjectivity of nature would thus work to oppose actions that tend to extinguish nonhuman species. Treating nature as a potential *speaking* subject also has its benefits. It allows nonhuman species a (type of) voice within the confines of human discourse, giving them a "presence" they might not otherwise enjoy. In the Kiva of Elders and the Council of All Beings, the purported interests of nonhuman species, as voiced by human understudies, are arguably more "present" than when represented by, for example, the utilitarian mythos of the so-called Wise Use movement.

My own view is that the move to recognize the nonhuman speaking subject, though motivated by admirable ethical concerns, is inevitably nagged by epistemological difficulties, which ultimately suggests that an ecocentric ethic is poorly served by such a strategy. At issue is the degree to which humans may be said to comprehend the interests of nonhuman entities as well as the ability of humans to "represent" such interests faithfully. A more comprehensive analysis of language and language use, following the linguistic theory proposed by Kenneth Burke, suggests that human apprehension of the nonhuman is mediated, and to a certain extent distorted, by the symbolic operations of language. Burke also complicates the "voice of nature" debate by differentiating between language as "symbolic action" and the critical processing of information, the former being the province of humanity and the latter of all physiological entities, to one degree or another. But whereas humanists ennoble the human species on the basis of such a distinction, Burke argues that linguistic ability, and specifically language as symbolic action, is not the unmitigated boon that the proponents of nonhuman linguistic subjectivity seem to assume. Indeed, for Burke, language is both "privilege" and "calamity," and as such it is not something we should necessarily wish upon our nonhuman kin, however "green" our motives.[4]

Knowledge, Symbolicity, and the Gift of Language

In *Language as Symbolic Action,* Burke tacitly evokes the Protagoras Myth by defining Man (in part) as "the symbol-using (symbol-making, symbol misusing) animal" (16). His theory of language as "symbolic action" depends explicitly upon an ontological distinction between one uniquely symbol-wielding species and the balance of creation. Just as, in the Protagoras Myth, humanity is dissociated from the rest of nature by virtue of the gift of language, Burke points out that man is "separated from his natural condition by instruments of his own making" (16). He asks:

> [S]ince language derives its materials from the cooperative acts of men in sociopolitical orders, which are themselves held together by a vast network of verbally perfected meanings, might it not follow that man must perceive nature through the fog of symbol-ridden social structures that he has erected atop of nature? (378)

Burke's assessment of the effect symbols have on our perception and representation of nature is typically ambiguous. For the "fog of symbol-ridden social structures" is, on Burke's account, not wholly obscuring. Symbolicity entails what he refers to as the "fatal fact" that

> all members of our species conceive of reality somewhat roundabout, through the various *media* of symbolism. Any such medium will be, as you prefer, either a way of "dividing" us from the "immediate" . . . or it can be viewed as a paradoxical way of "uniting" us with things on a "higher level of awareness," or some such. (52)

While I have introduced Burke here to remind us of the role language plays in human perception and cognition, I do not mean to suggest that proponents of "speaking nature" are necessarily insensitive to the vicissitudes of symbolicity, which Burke underlines, or the epistemological challenge such an analysis poses to human understanding of nonhuman interests. For his part, Murphy seems well aware of these issues. For example, he expresses concern for the prospects of nonhuman participation in democratic discourse, at least as articulated by Snyder. "I don't share his optimism about the facility of this move," says Murphy, although he continues to "believe in its necessity" ("Feminism" 50). Murphy argues, finally, that "the point is not to speak for nature, but to work to render the significance presented us by nature into verbal depiction by means of speaking subjects, whether this is through characterization in the arts or through discursive prose" (49).

Murphy emphasizes the fact that the nonhuman does gain a kind of presence in our discourse when we listen to the "voice" of nature and represent what we "hear" in terms of a quasi-subjectivity. He asserts, "Nonhuman others can be constituted as speaking subjects rather than merely objects of our speaking, although even the latter is preferable to silence" (50). In a sense, Murphy's strategy illustrates Burke's attitude toward symbolicity; while the "voice of nature" is ultimately a human construct that "overlays," and to a certain extent distorts, nonhuman nature, it can serve, if Snyder, Stone, and Murphy are correct, to connect us with the nonhuman "on a higher level of awareness." As Murphy indicates, he would rather take his chances with an instrumental "voice of nature" and its attendant epistemological problems than accept the continued silence and silencing of the nonhuman.

Lawrence Buell reaffirms Murphy's position when he says, "The rhetoric of nature's personhood speaks merely to the nominal level; what counts is the underlying ethical orientation implied by the troping" (217). He argues that we lose a strategic rhetorical resource when we abandon anthropomorphism entirely. "Yet to ban the pathetic fallacy—were such a thing possible—would be worse than to permit its unavoidable excesses. For without it, environmental care might not find its voice. For some, it might not even come into being" (218).

Murphy and Buell have a point. The epistemological concerns that accompany symbolic action may ultimately be subordinate to an ethical orientation. At a time when the silencing of the nonhuman facilitates its devastation, what seems to matter most is "presenting" the nonhuman within human discourse in a way that counters destructive attitudes and behavior. If the trope of speaking nature serves to oppose environmental destruction by positing a nonhuman subject with discursive, and moral, considerability, then writers who exploit it may at least be said to be engaged in a practical response to environmental crisis.

However we may regard the utility of the trope of speaking nature, two additional and interrelated problems complicate its use. In the first place, as authors move toward recognizing linguistic competency in the nonhuman subject, they tend both to overstate and understate significant distinctions among types of language use. Second, a careful consideration of these distinctions suggests that linguistic competency, at least in terms of symbolic action, is a mixed blessing, one that attenuates the satisfaction we might feel in recognizing such competency in the nonhuman subject.

As I noted at the outset, the trope of speaking nature is a poetic commonplace. The fact that poets are so often inclined to exploit anthropomorphism in the direction of oral linguistic competency is significant in and of itself; we seem to want to deal with the nonhuman literally in terms we understand, within the scope of human *parole*. The trope of speaking nature is thus supremely *anthropomorphic* in that nonhuman linguistic ability is modeled after human linguistic forms: the nonhuman as *rhetor*.

Some writers, perhaps uncomfortable with the unblushing anthropomorphism of, for example, Stafford's talking seed, retain the sense of linguistic competency in the nonhuman by construing such competency as independent of human *parole*. This strategy attempts to be nonanthropomorphic and ecocentric to the extent that it broadens the scope of language beyond the confines of human usage. Thus we may encounter the "voice of nature" speaking in a tongue we struggle to comprehend, as in Linda Hogan's poem "Naming the Animals":

> After the words that called legs, hands,
> the body
> of man out of clay and sleep,
> after the forgotten clay of his beginnings,
> after nakedness and fear of something larger,
> these he named: wolf, bear, other
> as if they had not been there
> before his words, had not
> had other tongues and powers
> or sung themselves into life
> before him.
>
> These he sent crawling into wilderness
> he could not enter,
> swimming into untamed water.

He could hear their voices at night
and tracks and breathing
at the fierce edge of the forest
where all things know the names for themselves
and no man speaks them
or takes away their tongue.

His children would call us pigs.
I am a pig,
the child of pigs,
wild in this land
of their leavings,
drinking from water that burns
at the edge of a savage country
of law and order.
I am naked, I am old
before the speaking,
before any Adam's forgotten dream,
and there are no edges to the names,
no beginning, no end.
From somewhere I can't speak or tell,
my stolen powers
hold out their hands
and sing me through.

(*The Book of Medicines* 40–41)

Hogan challenges the hubris of Western humanism, especially as it pertains to linguistic competency. She links the "silencing" of nature with the forces of conquest and environmental destruction. The "he" of the poem, an Adamic figure who is the product of (divine) verbal fiat, lays claim to the power of naming, creating distinct categories of beings ("wolf, bear"). Moreover, because his categories are distinctive, they perform the verbal magic of separating entities and, in the process, the self from the "other."

The speaker of the poem lays into the verbal arrogance of the Adamic character, pointing out that "he" goes about naming the animals "as if they had not been there / before his words, had not / had other tongues and powers / or sung themselves into life / before him." The arrogance of the Adamic character thus lies in his equation of his own verbal prowess with the verbal power of God which supposedly brings entities (like the Adamic character himself) to life. The speaker emphasizes that not only do the animals exist independently of the Adamic character's linguistic enthusiasm, but also they have their own speech and "powers" that allow them to sing themselves into existence, notably "before him."

Seemingly tormented by the animals' autonomy, and particularly by their "unauthorized" voices, the Adamic character banishes them into the wilderness, a place he cannot control and into which "he could not enter." In an important sense, the wilderness is yet another verbal construct, reflecting the boundary between what the Adamic character can create, and control, through his own speech, and that which lies beyond his verbal command. He is made anxious by the voices issuing from "the fierce edge of the forest" at night, "where all things know the names for themselves / and no man speaks them / or takes away their tongue."

In the final stanza the speaker contemplates the verbal legacy of the Adamic character, asserting, "His children would call us pigs," traditionally a "dirty" animal whose flesh is forbidden in some biblical traditions. For a moment the speaker accepts the label: "I am a pig / the child of pigs." As a typically "domesticated" animal, the speaker/pig crosses over into the sphere of human culture and language only to find a devastated landscape. Inverting the conventional association of nature with the primitive and barbaric, the pig describes the human sphere in ironic terms as a "savage country / of law and order."

But the name falls easily away, and by the end of the poem the speaker is "naked" once again, free of the effects of "law and order" that confine beings within firm linguistic boundaries. In the space beyond human naming, where "there are no edges to the names, / no beginnings, no end," the speaker recovers that which humanity claimed for itself: "From somewhere I can't speak or tell, / my stolen powers / hold out their hands / and sing me through." These "stolen powers" are explicitly cast in terms of verbal (and musical) ability, but Hogan is careful to preserve the sense that the voice of the animals operates according to different linguistic rules, beyond speaking and telling, beyond the hard edges of definition and difference.

While Hogan's poem focuses on recovering the autonomous voice of nature, nonhuman linguistic competency can also be construed in terms of written language, the ability to create and interpret "written" texts. Snyder carries this notion toward its logical, and ecocentric, extreme when claiming, "Other orders of beings have their own literature":

> Narrative in the deer world is a track of scents that is passed on from deer to deer with an art of interpretation which is instinctive. A literature of blood-stains, a bit of piss, a whiff of estrus, a hit of rut, a scrape on a sapling, and long gone. (*Practice* 112)

Snyder goes on to speculate, how solemnly it is difficult to determine, that "there might be a 'narrative theory' among these other beings—they might ruminate on 'intersexuality' or 'decomposition criticism'" (112). While he may be winking at us here, Snyder's point is serious inasmuch as it invites us to reconsider our traditional notions of linguistic competency. It does seem to be the case that many nonhuman species are, in a very catholic sense, "text producers," and that all beings are dependent, to one extent or another, on their ability to "read" and respond to their environment. If language use is, at base, the process of interpreting "texts" (whether leaves of grass or *Leaves of Grass*), then Snyder is correct to argue that humans are hardly the only linguistically competent species.

For his part, Burke would agree that all species interpret "texts" in some fashion. He says, "[A]ll organisms are critics in the sense that they interpret the signs about them" (*Permanence* 6). But is the production and interpretation of signs or "texts" all there is to language use? While it may be the goal of ecocentric writers to remove linguistic competency as the sign of human election, reducing language use to sheer hermeneutics arguably elides significant distinctions among types of linguistic behavior.

Burke makes the vital observation that human language use is uniquely *meta*-linguistic:

> Though other animals may manifest the rudiments of language or of tool-using, man's distinctive genius is in his capacity for doing things at one reserve, as when he uses words about words and makes tools for making tools. (*Permanence* 276 n)

It is thus the "reflexive or second-level aspect of human symbolism" that distinguishes human linguistic competency. Burke argues that, by virtue of its "reflexive" nature, language as *symbolic* action differentiates human language use from the even more complex "linguistic" behaviors of some nonhuman species. For example, he maintains that his analysis

> would presumably apply also to such complex sign systems as bees apparently have, to spread information about the distance and direction of a newly discovered food supply. Apparently, investigators really have "cracked" such a code in certain dancelike motions of bees—but we should hardly expect even to find that student bees are taught the language by teacher bees, or that there are apiaries where bees formulate the grammar and syntax of such signaling. "Information" in the sense of sheer motion is not thus "reflective," but rather is like that of an electric circuit where, if a car is on a certain stretch of track, it automatically turns off the current on the adjoining piece of track, so that any car on that other piece of track would stop through lack of power. The car could be said to behave in accordance with this "information." (*Language* 14)

According to Burke, then, we can distinguish between what we might call, on the one hand, sheerly "critical" behavior, the processing of "information" or, in more textual terms, the "interpretation" of "signs" and "signals," and, on the other hand, the manipulation of "symbols" ("words about words," "criticism of criticism")—the former being a universal characteristic of "language" writ large, the latter being the particular operation of language that identifies human language use as, in Burke's account, *symbolic* action.

While Burke's distinction between "criticism" and "symbolic action" depends on an understanding of the "reflexive" quality of symbolicity, it is also implied in his more fundamental ontological discrimination between the realms of motion and action. According to Burke, the sheerly physiological aspect of existence is the realm of *motion*. "Action," by contrast, "would involve modes of behaviour made possible by the acquiring of a conventional, arbitrary symbol system" ("[Nonsymbolic]" 809). Thus Burke concludes,

> So far as is known at present, the only typically symbol-using animal existing on earth is the human organism.
>
> The intuitive signaling systems in such social creatures as bees and ants would not be classed as examples of symbolic action.
>
> They are not conventional, arbitrary symbol systems such as human speech, which is not inborn but has to be learned, depending upon where the child happens to be "thrown," an accident of birth that determines whether the child learns Chinese, or French, or whatever idiom may prevail in the given locality. (810)

Because action is, by definition, symbolic, the realm of motion, which encompasses all nonhuman species, is accordingly *nonsymbolic* in nature.

In considering Burke's somewhat tautological distinction between symbolic and nonsymbolic language use, we may begin to detect the odor of humanism's self-aggrandizing accounts of human linguistic facility. We should note, however, that Burke is careful not to elevate humans on the basis of their aptitude for symbolicity. The fact that Burke explicitly refuses to do so is due, in large measure, to his lifelong concern with the ways in which symbolic action facilitates man's inhumanity to man (and to the nonhuman). The trouble with symbolic action can be traced to what Burke calls the "entelechial principle": the idea that there is a kind of inertia that governs the use of terms along certain lines according to an internal logic. According to Burke, many of our observations

> *are but implications of the particular terminology in terms of which the observations are made.* In brief, much that we take as observations about "reality" may be but the spinning out of possibilities implicit in our particular choice of terms. (*Language* 46; original emphasis)

The "entelechial principle" has as its more external or psychological counterpart what Burke calls the "principle of perfection": "A given terminology contains various *implications,* and there is a corresponding 'perfectionist' tendency for men to attempt carrying out those implications" (19; original emphasis). The motive of "perfection" necessitates, in dialectical fashion, the identification of concomitant terms of "imperfection," a process Burke calls "scapegoating." At its most extreme level of operation, scapegoating manifests itself as the tragedy of war, which claims real, rather than merely symbolic, victims. These victims can be human, as in the case of the "perfection" of racial identity and the extermination of "impure" members of the species, or they can be nonhuman. Burke points out that

> it would be an error to assume that the principle of victimage is confined to strictly personal forms. Not only animals, but even inanimate nature can serve as "perfect victim" in one situation or another. Some engineers, for instance, seem to have a "bulldozer mentality" and are never quite happy unless plotting roads through areas that require the destruction of great trees, as solemn as cathedrals. (39)

The "principle of perfection" thus motivates a range of symbolic action with the potential for tragic consequences in both the human and nonhuman spheres, which is why Burke adds, as the final codicil to his "Definition of Man," the assertion that, as the uniquely symbol-using, symbol-making, symbol-misusing animal, we are "rotten with perfection" (16).

Given the potential for "scapegoating" that symbolic action in some sense necessitates (although it may remain on the sheerly symbolic or "abstract" level), Burke is unwilling to glorify human linguistic competency:

> The designation of man as the symbol-using animal parallels the traditional formulas, "rational animal" and *Homo sapiens*—but with one notable difference. These earlier versions are honorific, whereas the idea of symbolicity implies no such temptation to self-flattery, and to this extent is more admonitory. (9)

Burke's linguistic analysis thus allows for differentiating between human and nonhuman linguistic competency, thereby taking into account the unique aspects of language as symbolic action, without succumbing to the temptation of linguistic vanity. In one of his more spirited passages, Burke says:

> We can distinguish man from other animals without being necessarily over-haughty. For what other animals have yellow journalism, corrupt politics, pornography, stock market manipulators, plans for waging thermonuclear, chemical, and bacteriological war? I think we can consider ourselves different in kind from the other animals, without necessarily being overproud of our distinction. We don't need theology, but merely the evidence of our characteristic sociopolitical disorders, to make it apparent that man, the typically symbol-using animal, is alas! something special. (50)

Burke's critique of symbolicity may be moot, however, if we are satisfied to follow Snyder's lead and accept a definition of nonhuman linguistic competency that avoids the difficulties entailed by symbolic action. In other words, nonhuman subjects can enjoy the gift of language and the status of language-bearers without being dogged by the liabilities of symbolicity. But in embracing this strategy we effectively sacrifice the possibility for nonhuman participation in human discourse, and especially democratic discourse, the ostensible goal of some "speaking nature" proponents. Humans and nonhumans may bear language equally, but lacking the ability to enter human discursive practices, nonhuman entities remain segregated by linguistic incommensurability.

We might do well, at this point, to question whether the overarching strategy of identifying humans and nonhumans in terms of linguistic competency is in fact the best way to establish a more heterarchical, ecocentric relationship. From a certain perspective, the attempt to recognize the nonhuman subject as linguistically competent strikes one as an essentially colonizing move. While it is true that claims to linguistic superiority have been used to enforce regimes of human supremacy, it does not necessarily follow that a more egalitarian relationship between humans and nonhumans depends on some notion of linguistic equality. Indeed, it is troubling that the ecocentric desire for equality encourages the erasure of what may be a real and significant difference between species. In the final section of this chapter, I examine the necessity for linguistic identification and consider the potential for a democratic and ecocentric practice that works to preserve linguistic differences.

Alinguistic Agency and Radical Democracy

In her analysis of the "speaking nature" controversy, Catriona Sandilands points out that efforts to recognize the voice of nature are modeled after a politics of identity that informs a variety of democratic struggles. These social movements are concerned with the liberation of oppressed classes primarily through their opposition to deployments of power that marginalize and silence. Once the forces of oppression begin to disintegrate, however, such movements face the problem of identifying the "authentic" voice of the oppressed class. Who speaks for Native Americans? for Tibetans? for gays or lesbians? Ecocritics attempting to recognize the nonhuman linguistic subject confront a similar problem. Who, or what, can speak for a tree, a pack, a swarm, a watershed, an ecosystem? According to Sandilands, the ecocritic faces the most basic of questions: "what is the authentic voice of nature?" (77).

Unless we take the position that human-nonhuman interlocution is a real possibility and not just an ecocentric fantasy, the fact is that the "voice of nature" problem is inherently different from other "authenticity of voice" quandaries. While there is always the possibility that oppressed humans, if given the opportunity, can learn to participate in democratic discourse, Sandilands maintains, correctly I believe, that we cannot simply count on the oppressed voice of nature to speak for itself (77–78). And when humans attempt to "speak for" nonhuman entities, they engage the epistemological problems inherent in symbolicity and perception. Sandilands observes, in a statement that resonates with Burke's own linguistic analysis:

> It is . . . important to note that all environmental discourse contains a moment of filtration, some point where nature is made knowable and meaningful; these are not merely convenient descriptive fictions, but carry important implications for the proscribed relations between humans and nonhuman nature. (76)

But rather than regarding the inability of the nonhuman subject to participate in democratic discourse, whether directly or by proxy, as a failure that subverts the possibility of emancipation, Sandilands argues that the *recognition* of this dilemma can serve as the basis for reconceptualizing democratic practices and our notions of the democratic subject upon which these social movements are based.

Thus far we have concerned ourselves with the ways in which the nonhuman subject may be said to be a language-bearer. According to Sandilands, the problems that this move elicits are not primarily problems of *language* but rather are problems of *subjectivity*, or at least subjectivity as construed in current political struggles. She argues:

> The process of the subjectivation of nature is impossible, in the terms of argument cast by contemporary social movement politics of identity: there cannot be an authentic voice of nature without profound revision of either the notion of speech or the notion of the speaking subject. The "I" that speaks in environmental discourse generally does not speak as the subject in these terms: it is always "something else," subject to a process of translation through other identities, through other forms of language. (78–79)

Since attempts to reconceptualize the notion of speech, and of linguistic competency in general, have so far failed to expedite the inclusion of nonhuman interests in democratic discourse in an epistemologically (and ethically) satisfactory manner, we may conclude, with Sandilands, that it is instead the idea of the "speaking subject" that invites further interrogation.

Sandilands points out that, because of the influence of social-movement identity politics on environmental discourse, the *subject* of nature

> has emerged as a *democratic* subject position, conditioned by notions of democracy already present in the other social movement struggles with which it is articulated. These notions of democracy have been strongly shaped by ideas emphasizing the need to value those identities repressed by the dominant culture, through the creation of new codes and meanings, new modes of speech from those repressed identities, to represent and construct alternative, liberatory ways of

> being in the world for that oppressed group. Democracy is thus viewed as being contingent not just on the ability to speak, but also on the mode of speech itself. (84–85)

But because humans cannot, in principle, identify the "authentic voice of nature," the ecological movement serves as a counterpoint to other democratic struggles by demonstrating the limits of identity politics. "Speaking as animals or speaking as nature is a project grounded in strong notions of democracy and liberation," notes Sandilands, "but its fundamental impossibility suggests the necessity of alternative configurations" (86).

Ecology points to the need for a more progressive democratic practice by revealing the limitations implicit in the idea of the democratic subject. Put another way, ecology demands that our democratic practices be revised because of the recognition (made possible by the failure of progressive social movements, including environmentalism, to identify an "authentic voice") that the subject, by virtue of the linguistic processes that produce it, is nonidentical to the Other it ostensibly represents. The primary value of environmental discourse is thus its potential to shift the ambition of progressive politics away from the search for articulate democratic subjects and toward an acceptance of discursive antagonism, in the form of nonidentity and pluralism, as fundamental to the democratic project. Or, as Sandilands puts it:

> [E]cology has us reexamine the subject of politics: it calls into question, in an urgent and profound way, the possibility of full human self-constitution as a political project. Thus, it shifts the basis of politics away from a quest for a speaking subject, a bearer of revolutionary consciousness, toward an understanding that this subject cannot possibly exist and that social change is based on this impossibility, this inherent self-limit. This recognition means that political actors cannot rely on a speaking subject to produce a new truth, be it a truth of nature or one emanating from any particular set of experiences, but

> must instead shoulder the responsibility for constituting a society that validates plurality as permanently unfixed and that recognizes ambiguity. (88–89)

What, then, would a democratic practice that "validates plurality as permanently unfixed and that recognizes ambiguity" look like? In attempting to formulate a more progressive articulation of democratic practices, Sandilands turns to a model of "radical democracy" suggested by Ernesto Laclau and Chantal Mouffe. According to Mouffe, radical democracy requires the proliferation of democratic struggles to produce what she calls a "hegemony of democratic values" (89). Radical democracy is thus grounded not in static notions of subjectivity or discourse but instead in antagonisms inherent to democratic practices. According to Sandilands, it is thus "a more profoundly democratic practice,"

> one which is concerned with destabilizing, on a variety of levels, the authority of a voice that claims to speak the truth of nature—or any other "truth"—in ways that are, at their core, antidemocratic and disempowering. Finding new ways to configure the subject of environmentalism rests on a process of reinventing ourselves, not as speaking subjects, but as actors in democratization; it is the process, not the authenticity of any particular form of speech, that will deepen the democratic possibilities for the ecological society toward which we strive. (90–91)

Having considered in some detail Sandilands's analysis of the "voice of nature" and the potential for a "radical democracy," where are we? Sandilands suggests that the egalitarian inclination of ecocentrism is perhaps better served by a redefinition of democratic values rather than the quest for the nonhuman speaking subject. By introducing the idea of "radical democracy," Sandilands opens up the theoretical possibility of a democratic practice that affords a variety of "subject" positions, including the position of "alinguistic subject" (though the term gets tangled in its own traces). In a sense, Sandilands's critique of democratic practices informed by contemporary identity politics generates an ontological category that Burke would have considered a contradiction in terms: the realm of "nonsymbolic action." Such a realm includes entities whose linguistic capabilities, if any, exclude symbolicity, but who also are construed to have interests and motives that deserve consideration in human discourse.[5]

A radical democratic practice that seeks to recognize the alinguistic "subject" must develop a new ontological and relational rhetoric. Ecological discourse, and other social movements, have begun this process. The revision of democratic practices can follow the lead of Donna Haraway who recommends replacing the rhetoric of subjectivity with a rhetoric of "agency." Following Bruno Latour, Haraway suggests that

> all sorts of things are actors, only some of which are human language-bearing actors, and that you have to include, as sociological actors, all kinds of heterogenous entities. I'm aware that it's a risky business, but this imperative helps to break down the notion that only the language-bearing actors have a kind of agency. Perhaps only those organized by language are *subjects*, but agents are more heterogenous. Not all the actors have language. (Penley and Ross 3)

A democratic practice that places a premium on agency, rather than subjectivity, would, in theory at least, take into account the interests of entities whose particular linguistic skills do not allow them to participate in democratic discourse, or who lack linguistic skills altogether. Just how such "accounting" is to proceed, however, is a rather murky business. Perhaps the first step is the most crucial: the recognition that, in principle, human and nonhuman alinguistic agents have interests not subordinate to the interests of the linguistically competent. Whether this kind of recognition would give alinguistic agents enough of a presence in democratic discourse to contest, to any significant degree, ongoing oppression and annihilation remains an open question.

From the standpoint of environmental poetics, however, it is clear that an ecocentric ethic is better served by aesthetic strategies that eschew the nonhuman speaking subject in favor of a rhetoric of alinguistic agency. In the next chapter I will explore just how such a rhetoric might be pursued. In the process, I hope to demonstrate in more detail how the limitation of identity, and the preservation of difference, remain at the heart of an environmental poetic practice.

May we not bear false witness to ourselves
About our neighbors,
Prophesying falsely
Why they did as they did.

—KENNETH BURKE, "Dialectician's Hymn"

CHAPTER 3

Ethos and Environmental Ethics

Environmental Representation and Ethos

As noted in the preceding chapter, the subject of nature has emerged as a site of contention in the discourse of environmental ethics. Catriona Sandilands has argued that the subject of nature has generally been constructed according to the logic of identity politics advanced by progressive social movements. The conception of democracy embraced by these movements generates a subject that is not only linguistically competent but also situated within a particular political and rhetorical matrix, one that emphasizes

> the need to value those identities repressed by the dominant culture, through the creation of new codes and meanings, new modes of speech from those repressed identities, to represent and construct

> alternative, liberatory ways of being in the world for that oppressed group. (84–85)

John Tallmadge's characterization of the subject of nature as "an oppressed and silent class, in need of spokespersons," exemplifies perfectly the influence of identity politics in the rhetoric of the natural subject (Buell 20–21). The question begged by Tallmadge's characterization is, of course, how can, or should, human beings "speak for" nature? To pose such a question is to begin to engage the full range of epistemological and ethical issues that attend the concept of "representation."

Thus far I have explored two very different strategies for representing what has been referred to variously as nature, the nonhuman, and the environment. In chapter 1, I examined a poetics derived from the principles of scientific and normative ecology. In chapter 2, I considered the potential subjectivity of nature, especially as such subjectivity is construed in terms of linguistic competency. These strategies present distinct conceptions of the human/nature relationship with correspondingly different roles for both sides of the "equation." In chapter 1, for example, I argued that a strictly ecologized poetic risks recapitulating the epistemological excesses that arguably precipitate environmental crisis and that ecology seeks to displace. In chapter 2, I argued that the attempt to reconceptualize the human/nonhuman dynamic in terms of linguistic intersubjectivity does less to establish a coherent and viable subject position for the nonhuman than it does to compel a redefinition of democratic subjectivity and democratic practice.

To be a "spokesperson" for nature is perhaps to claim still other roles for humans and nonhumans to play in environmental discourse. The term is preeminently ambiguous, allowing for very different rhetorical and ethical stances. There is the sense, first of all, that a "spokesperson" for nature is one who *speaks as* the nonhuman. In this case, the "representations" of the spokesperson are taken to "reflect" the will, desires, interests, and so on of the nonhuman. Again, since democratic practices powerfully influence how we conceive of such relations, we might logically expect such representatives to be "elected" or "appointed" in some fashion. But in the absence of parliamentary procedure, humans tend to "volunteer" for such duty. Consider, for example, Max Oelschlaeger's description of the relationship between nature and poet: "Wild nature will fable (from *fabulari*, to talk), that is, speak through a person if that person will but let natural phenomena have voice, and such a speaking will be as if literally true, alive, and organic ("Wilderness" 279). Here, Oelschlaeger suggests that one becomes a representative of "wild nature" simply by making oneself available to the "voice of nature."

Of course, this kind of vatic environmental poetics incurs the epistemological critique offered in the previous chapter. How do we know when, or if, the poet is speaking authentically, that is, truly representing nature's voice or voicing the truth about nature? If the "authentic voice of nature" is a fiction or an impossibility, what are the prospects for a poetics that seeks to represent it?

The second sense of "spokesperson" would seem to avoid some of these difficulties. The idea is that one *speaks for* the nonhuman by *speaking on its behalf*. The rhetorical stance implied by this second definition is one of *advocacy* rather than *representation* (in the political sense). In effect, being a "spokesperson" in this second sense is to acknowledge that one's representations, while ostensibly "faithful" to nonhuman interests, are nevertheless nonidentical with those interests.

A poetics structured by the first sense of "spokesperson" construes the task of representing nature as a mimetic project in the crudest sense of the term: mimesis as "copying" or "mirroring." By opening up to nature's voice, the poet is able to channel or "reflect" that voice into poetic discourse. But as Wolfgang Iser reminds us, representation as mimesis is always more than the act of producing a copy, as even Aristotle acknowledged:

> In the Aristotelian sense, the function of representation is twofold: (1) to render the constitutive forms of nature perceivable; and (2) to complete what nature has left incomplete. In either case mimesis, though of paramount importance, cannot be confined to mere imitation of what is, since the processes of elucidation and of completion both require a performative activity if apparent absences are to be moved in to presence. ("Play" 249)

To *speak as* and to *speak on behalf of* nature are equivalent practices, however, inasmuch as they invoke both elucidation and completion. Oelschlaeger acknowledges the importance of the second function of mimesis in nature poetry when he says:

> The thinking poet reaches toward a presence obscured by the obvious, toward what is absent or missing because of its concealment behind language, behind opinion, behind the governing ideology that rules the world: *the wilderness poet calls forth Being.* ("Wilderness" 299, original emphasis)

In depicting aspects of the natural world, the "thinking poet" thus "imitates" nature at the same time as he or she "completes" our understanding by representing (re-presenting) what in nature would otherwise remain absent.

Iser points out that in English the term *representation* tends to elide the crucial difference between the two senses of mimesis. He argues that by conflating "elucidation" and "completion" we conceal "the performative qualities through which the act of representation brings about something that hitherto did not exist as a given object." In addition, he argues that the German synonym *Darstellung* better captures the performative action of representation without "referring to any object given prior to the act of representation" ("Representation" 236). Similarly, Gayatri Spivak notes that German allows for a distinction between the two senses of representation: *Darstellung*, which she associates with "tropology" and the aesthetic "staging" of meaning ("completion" by the presentation of absences), and *Vertretung*, associated with persuasion and rhetoric (with heavy emphasis on substitution and displacement, as in political representation), though she ultimately questions the validity of the distinction (276–278).

The difference, then, between *speaking as* and *speaking on behalf of* is exhibited in the contrast between the two senses of mimesis and representation. What is important here is the fact that the two senses of mimesis and representation imply very different epistemological and ethical stances.

Oelschlaeger's contention that wild nature can "speak through" the poet implies a mimetic operation that allows nature to be "copied" or "translated" into poetic discourse free of the distorting effects of human perception and language. As I argued in the previous chapter, this kind of mimetic ambition ignores the vicissitudes of symbolic action as well as the proclivities of human cognition. On the other hand, the idea that the poet is able to make present an absent nature underscores the performative aspect of poetic representation. Even so, to the extent that the poet claims to have presented nature as it exists independent of the representative act, he or she remains vulnerable to a similar epistemological critique. That is to say, the "Being" called forth by the poet in poetry is essentially nonidentical to the "Being" that was "absent" before the act of representation.

There remains the theoretical possibility of a kind of representation that is both explicitly performative and acknowledges the contingency of the representative product. This is what Iser has in mind, I believe, when he embraces representation as *Darstellung*, as "aesthetic semblance." Representation as aesthetic semblance allows for the interplay of an extratextual world and the "fictionalizing" action of the literary text ("Representation" 237). Crucially, the notion of representation as aesthetic semblance requires us to recognize that representations of nature are always conditioned by the contingencies of the performances that produce them; in other words, they are the products of particular rhetorical strategies and rhetorical situations.[1] Furthermore, the status of the literary text as aesthetic semblance generates an essential tension between the meanings produced by the text and their contingency, a tension that can be resolved only by sacrificing the "fictionalizing action" that produces these meanings in the first place.

Although Iser is primarily interested in the "fictionalizing" aspects of representation in the novel (and in drama), I believe his insight into the literary text as aesthetic semblance applies equally to poetry if we approach poetry from the proper perspective. That perspective will be developed in some detail in the next chapter, with particular reference to Robert Frost's theory of metaphor. Suffice it to note here that the metaphorical action of poetry serves the same function as the "fictionalizing action" of the novel. If this is true, then we should be able to identify a poetry that treats of nature in terms of aesthetic semblance. As a first step, we will want to look for poetry that contests the notion that the significance of nature can be represented in largely unproblematic, or crudely mimetic, ways. Of particular interest will be the degree to which the poet claims to achieve the kinds of "identifications" by virtue of which his or her knowledge of the nonhuman is grounded. We will also concern ourselves with poetry that resists such "identifications," and with the ethical imperative to which such resistance arguably responds.

Negotiating the Environment: Readings

I

As we saw in chapter 2, one way poets construct their knowledge of nature is to "identify" with the nonhuman in ways that give access to the "authentic" experience of nature. Identification in terms of linguistic competency affords the opportunity for interspecies communication and thus the possibility of authentic knowledge of nonhuman experience, "from the horse's mouth," as it were.

In Norman Russell's "Message of the Rain" we can observe a rather standard deployment of this strategy:

> when i was a child
> i was a squirrel a bluejay a fox
> and spoke with them in their tongues
> climbed their trees dug their dens
> and knew the taste
> of every grass and stone
> the meaning of the sun
> the message of the night
> now i am old and past
> both work and battle
> and know no shame
> to go alone into the forest
> to speak again to squirrel fox and bird
> to taste the world
> to find the meaning of the wind
> the message of the rain
>
> (*Amicus Journal* 59)

Russell begins with the Romantic conceit of childhood as the arena for extraordinary knowledge and proceeds to push identification to its logical conclusion: "when i was a child / i was a squirrel a bluejay a fox / and spoke with them in their tongues." Radical identification ("i was a squirrel a bluejay a fox") entails the ability to communicate, to experience and understand existence *as* the nonhuman; likewise, the ability to communicate reinforces the identification desired in this poem: "[i] climbed their trees dug their dens / and knew the taste / of every grass and stone / the meaning of the sun / the message of the night." Russell construes aspects of nature (the sun, the night) as signifying entities and endows the "child" of the poem with the hermeneutical power to ascertain their significance.

The poem describes the recovery of this hermeneutical power (lost to adulthood) through the offices of language. The shameless elder, who is "past / both work and battle," ventures alone into the forest to reclaim the ability "to speak again to squirrel fox and bird." As in the "childhood" section of the poem, knowledge of the nonhuman is predicated on identification in terms of language. The order here is telling: proficiency in nonhuman language is followed by the speaker's ability "to taste the world / to find the meaning of the wind / the message of the rain."

What saves this poem from utter banality is the fact that Russell declines to deliver these "meanings" and "messages" to his reader. Having presented nature as the site of signification, Russell seems content to let his speaker rest assured in the knowledge he or she has recovered. To risk exposing that knowledge with any exactitude, however, would be to cancel the speaker's need for communication and language and, not incidentally, to suspend the motive for the poem itself. As it stands, this poem leaves the reader contemplating the significance of the natural world, having been encouraged to anticipate signification in the approach to nature. Or perhaps the reader is left to marvel at the pull of meaning itself, the allure of signification that motivates, and licenses, the tactics of identification.

II

In Mark Jarman's "Chimney Swifts," we can observe a very different attitude toward identification with the nonhuman, especially in terms of linguistic proficiency:

> Throughout the winter, we once believed, they hid
>   Nearby us, under eaves,
> In nestlike thatch and thickets wedged in tile,
> Sleeping as close to us as figures carved
>   On vaults and open rafters.

They were, in fact, skimming the Amazon.

They are back now, with cowbirds, boat-tailed grackles,
Kingbirds on powerlines,
And quick goldfinches heading for the fields
They drown their color in, in northern mountains.

Swifts funnel down at twilight
Into cold flues, chattering like children.

They speak their language and we listen
In our own, comparing them
To children, travellers, speed, and life itself,
Imparting a charmed knowledge unto us.

To them, there are two worlds—
The soot-thick shaft and the silky bowl of sky.

To watch for them, to become expectant,
To need their spring arrival,
To know the kink from craning back the neck
During the warm, late afternoons of April,
Is part of the enchantment,

Is to believe they feel it, too, and act.

(*Crazyhorse* 41 [Winter 1991] 70)

"Chimney Swifts" exposes the disjunction between what we imagine of the nonhuman and the ostensible truth of nonhuman existence. The speaker first introduces what turns out to be a fanciful explanation of where swifts reside in the winter. The image is intimate: "they hid / Nearby us, under eaves, / In nestlike thatch and thickets wedged in tile, / Sleeping as close to us as figures carved / On vaults and open rafters." The speaker is quickly disabused of this fantasy, however. Nevertheless, what is most interesting about this poem is the way in which it resists total demystification. When the voice of truth enters to correct the speaker's misconceptions ("They were, in fact, skimming the Amazon"), the effect is only a momentary suppression of imaginative and, we note, verbal play.

Undeceived now by the "fact" of the swifts' migration, the speaker goes on to recount, in fairly prosaic terms, the return of other types of migratory birds. The flat, descriptive diction ("They are back now, with cowbirds") is almost immediately disrupted, however, by the figure of the "boat-tailed grackles" and, later, by the image of the "quick goldfinches heading for the fields / They drown their color in, in northern mountains," with its quirky syntax and stunning visual impact. And in the next stanza, the speaker abandons the literal altogether in favor of a conspicuous simile: "Swifts funnel down at twilight / Into cold flues, chattering like children."

The tension between the literal and the figurative, between fact and fancy, is mirrored in the next stanza in the speaker's appraisal of the two "languages": "They speak their language and we listen / In our own, comparing them / To children, travellers, speed, and life itself." It is significant, I believe, that the speaker does not try to translate swift into human but instead emphasizes the incommensurability of the two "languages" and the way in which the imagination "translates" and transmutes the voice of nature into human figures. By preserving the linguistic distinction that obtains between the two species, the speaker allows the swifts a modicum of ontological autonomy. The knowledge that emerges into human language is thus "charmed" in the sense that the process of "translation" charges it with a necessary "mystery" (accentuated by the ritualistic, and somewhat archaic, "unto us"), which is captivating in the several senses of the word.

Having just insisted on the disjunction between human and swift languages, the speaker hazards a claim concerning how swifts purportedly regard the topography of their lives: "To them, there are two worlds— / The soot-thick shaft and the silky bowl of sky." The assertion is a bit jarring, assuming as it does a very intimate understanding of how swifts construct a sense of their environment. If we note, however, the metaphor embedded in the claim ("the silky bowl of sky") we might guess that the speaker is rather self-consciously underlining which language, and interpretive structure, remains at work here. We are thus invited to conclude, I believe, that the knowledge this claim addresses is also "charmed," refracted as it is through the figures of human language.

By the end of the poem, the speaker seems to exhibit a renewed commitment to the kind of "imaginative sympathy" that was impugned at the beginning of the poem by the voice of reason: "To watch for them, to become expectant, / To need their spring arrival, / To know the kink from craning back the neck / During the warm, late afternoons of April, / Is part of the enchantment, / Is to believe they feel it, too, and act." The speaker does not abandon skepticism entirely, however. Jarman carefully preserves the possibility that the speaker is "enchanted" in the negative sense, and that the whole spring ritual of identifying with the swifts on the level of common feeling and purpose might be nothing more than a solipsistic exercise. The poem's attitude is finally rather practical; whatever the truth might be concerning the swifts' experience, Jarman suggests that, by simply acting in a way that at least entertains the possibility of a reciprocal response from nature, the speaker has positively transformed his or her relationship to the nonhuman. Most notably, the speaker is able to regain a feeling of sympathetic association with nature, a benefit that ultimately outweighs the epistemological anxiety that linguistic and ontological difference produces in this poem.

III

In his poem "In the Bog behind My House," Ira Sadoff presents the idea of identification in an entirely different light. The danger here is that the speaker will succumb to the perils of too much identification.

The scene itself provokes anxiety; it is a place where one can get "bogged" down, trapped:

> The crows have come back for April
> and the first buds, the hyacinths.
> They leave winter for the hearty chickadees.
>
> They love the muddy ditches
> dressed with possums, mice, and skunks.
> Crows find the mist inviting, the fog banks
>
> where deer have been slumbering—wounded deer
> who limped through winter. We could say
> crows are cynical, shadows on the wall, our wings
>
> flapping, our jaws chewing with a sudden fury.
> We could say the sound of crows is a chasm.
> The way I see the bog behind my house
>
> it is always April. It is always April
> when I feel the sheen of black and blue.
> When I hear them picking clean the sparrow wings.
>
> God, teach me how to love the crows
> for being crows, to care for those
> the crows won't spare, without becoming them.

Danger, and attraction, emanate from the crows who return to the bog in April to take advantage of its "muddy ditches / dressed with possums, mice, and skunks." They take advantage, too, of the "inviting" mist and "the fog banks / where deer have been slumbering—wounded deer / who limped through winter." The speaker seems intimidated by the crows' unapologetic penchant for both opportunistic and insidious murder.

How to explain the crows? How to deal with the trepidation they produce? The speaker essays an explanation of sorts ("We could say / crows are cynical, shadows on the wall"), but the conditional mood frustrates the movement toward understanding. Having offered a tentative and seemingly ineffective rationalization for the crows' behavior, the speaker proceeds to collapse into identity: "*our* wings / flapping, *our* jaws chewing with a sudden fury" (emphasis mine). The speaker flounders for a moment before retreating back into the self, concluding (conditionally), "We could say the sound of the crows is a chasm." The speaker might mean here that the sound of the crows is a chasm into which he might fall, like the bog, his own voice subsumed by the collective and alien voice of the crows. Alternatively, the *sound* of the crows, explicitly *not* expressed in terms of voice, could be a chasm in the sense that its radical alterity *separates* the crows from the human and from the realm of human understanding.

Possessed now by the terror that the crows represent for him, the speaker endures a corrupted and eternal spring ("it is always April") that continually draws him into contact with his fear: "It is always April / when I feel the sheen of black and blue. / When I hear them picking clean the sparrow wings." The delicate brutality of the last image captures the speaker's dilemma perfectly. He seems attracted to the murderous efficiency of the crows at the same time as he is repulsed by their cruelty.

The poem ends with the speaker pleading for a way to negotiate this dilemma without losing himself in the process. He would like to both "love the crows / for being crows" and "to care for those / the crows won't spare, without becoming them." The last pronoun is wonderfully ambiguous. For to "love the crows / for being crows" would be to accept them in all their homicidal eminence, thus forfeiting the human perspective that allows the speaker to worry over their brutality and ruthlessness. Similarly, "to care for those / the crows won't spare" risks an anthropocentric coercion by judging the crows according to human ethical standards, effectively forcing the identification of crows and humans on human terms. Thus, in a brilliant twist, this last line of the poem sets one final trap for the speaker. By surrendering to the lure of anthropocentrism, the speaker becomes one of those whom "the crows won't spare," bogged down in (human) identity.

IV

Identification with the nonhuman is explicitly resisted in Peter Borrelli's poem "The River":

> The river, cold and dark as gun metal,
> white streamers advancing,
> rushes the gabions and riprap
> of the near shore.
>
> Sailboats tug and recoil
> at their moorings, their halyards
> and shackles jangling in the wind.
>
> Willows sway over the embankment,
> their long leaves raking the water.
>
> In the sheltered cove a night heron
> feeding among the reeds and hyacinth
> senses the coming violence and pauses.
>
> Its ruby eye meets mine
> with neither fear nor sympathy.
> We are not one
> but captured in the same moment.

After some fairly straightforward description, this poem moves toward a dramatic encounter between the speaker, arguably the poet in this case, and a "night heron." I am tempted to identify the speaker as the poet because the tension in the poem stems from the supposed "violence" of the moment of perception, which is also, for the poet, the moment of representation.

Reading the poem for the first time, however, we know only that the heron "senses the coming violence" without being sure of the nature of the threat. Interestingly, the heron elects to pause rather than flee. And the syntax of the next line, "Its ruby eye meets mine," as well as the choice of verb, "meets," also suggest a degree of volition on the part of the heron. The heron seems willing to engage the "coming violence" at least halfway.

The speaker of the poem is unable to get a fix on the heron's emotional response, noting only that the bird is experiencing "neither fear nor sympathy," presumably the two emotional extremes. The heron remains resolutely in place, and yet inscrutable, provocative in its obdurate alterity. As a result, the speaker can only conclude, "We are not one / but captured in the same moment."

The key question prompted by this poem would seem to be: what is the nature of the "coming violence"? One immediate and rather obvious answer is that the act of perception is itself a violent act, dividing the world along Cartesian lines into subject and objects. On this reading, the emotional valence of "We are not one" would be somewhat rueful. The valence of the verb "captured" also supports this reading. The speaker and the heron are united in perception only in the way that fellow prisoners may be said to be "united" in their common captivity.

A very different reading takes into better account what was dismissed as incidental scenery in the first. The title of the poem would also seem to insist on a different focus. The poem begins with "The river, cold and dark as gun metal / white streamers advancing, / rushes the gabions and riprap / of the near shore." The description of the river "dark as gun metal" suggests an alternative source of the "coming violence": the river itself. The list of powerful, kinetic verbs ("advancing," "rushes," "tug," "recoil," "jangling") also contributes to the sense of the river as a powerful force and potential danger.

Even so, the violence in this poem is in fact instigated not by the river but rather by the act of perception, as we saw in our first reading. What changes is the feeling of movement and energy. From the rushing river and its dynamic activity the poem slows, its movement restrained by less vigorous verbs ("Willows sway," "long leaves raking"). The violence is precipitated once the poem moves into the heron's "sheltered cove" and all activity collapses into the locked gaze.

The real violence in this poem thus seems to be the arresting of all activity in the moment of static vision. Without motion, the various actors in the poem cease their interactions and become isolated monads. Where once these actors were united by virtue of their interanimation (the river rocking the boats whose halyards and shackles jangle in the same wind that sways the willow whose leaves rake the river), now the speaker can correctly announce, "We are not one." And since it is the poem itself that ultimately "translates" the kinetic energy of the river into the static and fairly dull image of the heron and the speaker locked in mutual gaze, the real source of the violence is poetry and the real perpetrator is the poet. The poet's symbolic act results in a kind of "symbolic violence" by rendering the flux of the world in terms of the relatively static patterns of language.

Beyond Environmental Mimesis

All four of these poems negotiate the human/nonhuman relationship. The processes of identification and difference are crucial elements in these negotiations. In "The Message of the Rain," for example, Russell identifies humans (or at least some humans) and nonhumans in terms of shared linguistic competency. Through this identification, Russell allows his speaker access to the authentic experience of the nonhuman, even if the speaker is not permitted, by the poet or because of the aesthetic constraints of the poem, to articulate knowledge of this experience.

Epistemologies imply ethics. Russell's poem is colonizing to the extent that it figures the nonhuman as entirely knowable. Further, it is my contention that the move to identify the human and nonhuman in terms of linguistic competency is an essentially anthropocentric gesture. Such identification obliterates difference.[2] While identification is an integral aspect of discourse, a radically democratic interpretation of ecocentrism suggests the need for the interrogation of its operation.

In this context, Jarman's refusal to equate human and swift linguistic competency takes on ethical import. By respecting the distinction between the two "languages," Jarman allows for nonidentity in the human/nonhuman relationship. While he presents the swifts as language bearers, in contrast to Russell, he does not do so to provide access to authentic nonhuman experience of knowledge. Instead, Jarman uses the incommensurability of human and nonhuman linguistic competency as the site of his interrogation of identity and nonidentity. In "Chimney Swifts," the speaker's ability to achieve understanding of the nonhuman is divorced from the issue of language. Instead, it rests on the speaker's cultivation of a "sympathetic imagination." And though Jarman ultimately embraces the possibility of such sympathy, his faith is bracketed by an explicit critique of its epistemological ambiguity.

Sadoff's poem serves as an antidote to the assumption that identification with the nonhuman is intrinsically desirable. To become identified with the crows is not to frolic with them, as Russell's speaker frolics with the squirrel, bluejay, and fox, but rather to take on what appears, from the human perspective, to be a merciless modus operandi. As Sadoff indicates, the problem is how to "love" and "care" for beings that are radically different from us without collapsing into either absolute identity or absolute alterity. While Sadoff rather successfully stages this dilemma, he can offer no resolution to it.

In Borrelli's "The River," the tension between identity and nonidentity is brought home to the province of poetics. I have suggested that the poem enacts the "violence" of representation by transforming the dynamic interplay of the river into the static structure of language and poetry. The irony, of course, is that *both* the motion of the river and the stasis of the moment of perception are "captured" in the poem. Rereading the poem, fixing our gaze on it, we understand that the "coming violence" has already occurred.

The problem of identity and nonidentity thus returns us to the dilemma of representation. My reading of these poems begins to suggest the outlines of an environmental poetics less interested in representation as a way to call forth an absent nature than as the staging of our desire for identification. Such a poetics would move beyond mimesis toward an understanding of how representation both satisfies and frustrates our desire for identity. I will argue in the final two chapters that such a poetics can also serve ecocentric goals by integrating discursive and environmental ethical concerns.

May we compete with one another,
To speak for Thy creation with more justice—
Cooperating in this competition
Until our naming
Gives voice correctly,
And how things are
And how we say things are
Are one.

—KENNETH BURKE,
"Dialectician's Hymn"

CHAPTER 4

Pragmatic Environmental Poetics

Contemporaneity, Nature, and Knowledge

We know that Pope published the first epistle of his *Essay on Man* in March 1733. But could these lines have been written recently, say, at the beginning of the twenty-first century?

> See, through this air, this ocean, and this earth,
> All matter quick, and bursting into birth.
> Above, how high, progressive life may go!
> Around, how wide! how deep extend below!
> Vast chain of Being! which from God began,
> Natures ethereal, human, angel, man,
> Beast, bird, fish, insect, what no eye can see,
> No glass can reach; from Infinite to thee,
> From thee to Nothing.—On superior powers

> Were we to press, inferior might on ours:
> Or in the full creation leave a void,
> Where, one step broken, the great scale's destroyed:
> From Nature's chain whatever link you strike,
> Tenth, or ten thousandth, breaks the chain alike.
>
> (I.VIII)

I would like to ask this cheeky question as a way of posing, roundabout, a more general and knotty one: besides the date of composition, what is "contemporary" about the contemporary nature poem? The question is triggered, in the first instance, by the recent proliferation of anthologies of "contemporary nature poetry." It is provoked, too, by what I see as the challenge of writing nature poetry in an era in which the "idea" of nature, and the poet's ability to comprehend, and in some fashion represent, "nature," are susceptible to a panoply of skeptical critiques, even as the necessity for better representation becomes increasingly evident.

If we can set aside Pope's diction and the syntactic markers that signal the poem's eighteenth-century pedigree, we discover an argument that appears to resonate with aspects of contemporary ecological reasoning.[1] By appropriating the notion of creation as a "Vast chain of Being," for example, Pope embraces a view of nature as an integral, "amazing Whole," a perspective not inconsistent with ecological representations of nature as an amalgamation of interdependent and reciprocal systems and subsystems. Furthermore, Pope's sense of the sensitivity and fragility of natural relationships may strike the contemporary reader, well versed in the tragedies of environmental disaster (from Love Canal to Bhopal to the *Exxon Valdez*), as ecologically prescient: "Or in the full creation leave a void, / Where, one step broken, the great scale's destroyed: / From Nature's chain whatever link you strike, / Tenth, or ten thousandth, breaks the chain alike." In fact, the contemporary reader is probably more inclined to accept the possibility of wholesale environmental disintegration than Pope's original audience was, given the threat, unique to the twentieth century, of global devastation, whether nuclear, chemical, or biological in nature.[2]

We can compare Pope's description with E. O. Wilson's 1984 portrait of the interdependent and reciprocal relationships that obtain in a complex ecosystem:

> The woods were a biological maelstrom of which only the surface could be scanned by the naked eye. . . . But I knew that all around me bits and pieces, the individual organisms and their populations were working with extreme precision. A few of the species were locked together in forms of symbiosis so intricate that to pull out one would bring others spiraling to extinction. Such is the consequence of adaptation by coevolution, the reciprocal genetic change of species that interact with each other through many life cycles. Eliminate just one kind of tree out of hundreds in such a forest, and some of its pollinators, leafeaters, and woodborers will disappear with it, then various of their parasites and key predators, and perhaps a species of bat or bird that depends on its fruit—and when will the reverberations end? Perhaps not until a large part of the diversity of the forest collapses like an arch crumbling as the keystone is pulled away. (7–8)

Like Pope, Wilson anticipates cataclysmic results from relatively minor disruptions in the natural order, though he goes on to speculate that the effects are more likely to remain local, "ending with a minor shift in the overall pattern of abundance among the numerous surviving species." And just as Pope foresees catastrophe in human overreaching, Wilson acknowledges the sensitivity and fragility of natural systems, and our inability to discern more than superficial levels of interconnection, as an argument against meddling in the "biological maelstrom." The results of human intervention, concedes Wilson, "are beyond the power of present-day ecologists to predict." "It is enough to work on the assumption," he concludes, "that all of the details matter in the end, in some unknown but vital way" (8).

That the *Essay on Man* is ultimately a diatribe against human intellectual pride also accords well with another important aspect of contemporary ecological reasoning. Pope's argument in the *Essay on Man* is remarkably similar to David Erhenfeld's polemic in *The Arrogance of Humanism* against "the religion of humanism" and its "supreme faith in human reason—its ability to confront and solve the many problems that humans face, its ability to rearrange both the world of Nature and the affairs of men and women so that human life will prosper" (5). Erhenfeld argues that our faith in reason must be tempered by an understanding of its limitations, and in particular that our ambition to command and control nature must be abandoned if only in the name of intellectual humility.

Pope, too, is concerned with the consequences of intellectual pride. He counsels: "Know thy own point: This kind, this due degree / Of blindness, weakness, Heaven bestows on thee. / Submit" (I.X). Failure to submit, he suggests, threatens terrestrial if not cosmological disaster as it reveals our suicidal (and perhaps genocidal) arrogance: "All this dread ORDER break—for whom? for thee? / Vile worm!—Oh Madness! Pride! Impiety!" (I.VIII)

Erhenfeld's assault on humanism represents a key element in the renunciation of homocentric values and the development of a more ecocentric orientation, an attitude that contends that natural creation is essentially nonhierarchical and centerless. In offering his own critique of reason, Pope may also be said to lean toward the ecocentric. By positioning humanity in the thick of creation ("Above, how high, progressive life may go! / Around, how wide! how deep extend below!") rather than simply at its summit, and by offering his own critique of human reason, Pope introduces, and reinforces, an ecocentric alignment.

Despite these rather crude correspondences, Pope's *Essay on Man* can also be seen to cut across the contemporary grain. Though the metaphor of the "chain of Being" allows Pope to emphasize relational identities, the living bonds that link "Natures ethereal, human, angel, man, / Beast, bird, fish, insect, what no eye can see, / No glass can reach," it is also a metaphor that, in its vertical extension, establishes a strict ontological hierarchy. As Pope sees it, this hierarchy is indexed by intellectual (and "sensual") disparities that obtain among the different orders of Being. In the final analysis, however, rational power is reaffirmed as the sign of election: "Far as Creation's ample range extends, / The scale of sensual, mental powers ascends: / Mark how it mounts, to Man's imperial race, / From the green myriads in the peopled grass" (I.VII). Even though humanity's own stature is checked by the existence of superior beings (such as angels), such a hierarchy is doggedly homocentric, in that humanity is privileged above other species in the cosmic pecking order. If the contemporary current is moving toward ecocentrism, the *Essay on Man* clearly remains caught in a homocentric eddy.[3]

The radically democratic reasoning that makes possible an ecocentric orientation also works against the *Essay on Man*'s rather explicit aristocratic politics. As every textbook introduction to Pope inevitably points out, the cosmological stratification so zealously guarded by Pope also reinforces more mundane distinctions of class. Thus when Pope asks, "What if the foot, ordained the dust to tread, / Or hand, to toil, aspired to be the head? / What if the head, the eye, or ear repined / To serve mere engines to the ruling Mind?" (I.IX), it is difficult for the contemporary reader (or at least the contemporary reader with some allegiance to democratic traditions) not to hear Pope as an apologist for power and privilege. Pope's is the appeal of the Brahmin: "One truth is clear, Whatever is, is Right" (I.X).

While these observations are meant to suggest some of the similarities, and dissimilarities, between the *Essay on Man* and more contemporary attitudes, this cursory analysis should serve to suggest, most of all, the difficulties that the idea of contemporaneity conjures up. For inasmuch as contemporaneity tempts originality, it also summons the debts of the moment, as Eliot cryptically reminds us in "Burnt Norton":

> Time present and time past
> Are both perhaps present in time future,
> And time future contained in time past.
>
> (13)

Thus far I have attempted to assay the ostensible contemporaneity of the *Essay on Man* by identifying some of the rhetorical positions common to the early eighteenth and early twenty-first centuries. These arguments include Pope's quasi-holistic cosmology and his critique of intellectual arrogance. I have also tried to show where the *Essay on Man* stakes out positions that are more difficult to adapt to a contemporary frame of reference. These include the poem's aristocratic political commitments and their homocentric ramifications.

To fully appreciate the distance between the *Essay on Man* and the contemporary field of poetry, however, we need to focus less on the particular arguments at hand and more on the poetics that authorize them. To be clear, by *poetics* I mean specifically the theory of knowledge and representation that a poem or a poetry may be said to instantiate, whether explicitly or implicitly. Let us consider first the theory of knowledge that Pope demonstrates in the *Essay on Man*. What is most noticeable is the scope of the speaker's vision. Pope presents a comprehensive perspective ranging literally "from Infinite . . . to Nothing." It is a perspective that apprehends all of creation from the macroscopic (Planets, Suns, the spheres of Angels, Heaven itself) to the microscopic (at least as far as the level of insects, beyond which "no eye can see,/No glass can reach"). It is also a perspective that is finely tuned, able to discern the fine gradations that constitute the cosmological Order, the individual links in the Chain of Being.

In terms of what can be known, then, the *Essay on Man* is obviously ambitious. The irony, of course, is that we confront this ambition in a poem that explicitly targets intellectual overreaching. While confessing the limitations of human understanding, Pope is utterly certain of an Order that, though ostensibly beyond rational grasp, structures the cosmos and all relations therein: "All Nature is but Art, unknown to thee;/All Chance, Direction, which thou canst not see;/All Discord, Harmony not understood;/All partial Evil, universal Good" (I.X). Privy to apocalyptic vision, the speaker can see through to the ground of ultimate reality (while the rest of us remain pointedly bewildered).

Even so, to distinguish Pope's theory of knowledge, as I have begun to do, and his theory of representation is, in a crucial sense, to miss the point. I have referred to the vast "perspective" that the *Essay on Man* offers, but the scope of Pope's vision belies the term. Indeed, to speak of Pope's "theory of knowledge" is already to import the idea of perspective into a poem that ultimately insists on its own largely unfettered purview. As Kenneth Burke reminds us, a theory is literally "a *looking-at*, or *viewing*," a definition that underlines the conditioned, "perspectival" nature of theoretical approach (*Permanence* 125).[4] In the *Essay on Man*, knowledge of nature and the cosmos is not bracketed by Pope's approach to it; it is simply and absolutely autonomous.

Similarly, to call attention to Pope's "theory of representation" is in effect to trouble calm waters. The *Essay on Man* simply tells it like it is. The sign of Pope's confidence in his ability to represent the order of things is the perfect absence of representational anxiety.

The difference between the *Essay on Man* and a poetry that would admit theoretical concern is the difference between exegetical and hermeneutical poetics. It is a difference that can be explained in part by the social and literary history that estranges the contemporary field of poetry, in its most democratic aspect, from Pope's Neoplatonic surety. This history may be usefully understood largely in terms of an increasing pluralization of both civic and aesthetic space.

That is to say, the multiplication of voices in political and poetic discourse, and the differences (and principle of difference) they represent, call into question the authority of the single vision and the single voice presented in the *Essay on Man*. From an "evolutionary" perspective, exegetical poetics is displaced by hermeneutical poetics as the result of democratic reform.

Or perhaps democratic reform is the result of the inevitable disintegration of conceptual regimes. Burke puts it this way:

> Meaning or symbolism becomes a central concern precisely at that stage when a given system of meanings is falling into decay. In periods of firmly established meanings, one does not study them, one uses them: one frames his acts in accordance with them. (*Permanence* 162)

Pope is one who employs his system of meanings with supreme confidence; his *Essay on Man* is a rhetorical act framed in accordance with them. Poetry as exegesis. Once the solitary hold on meaning releases, however, symbolic action becomes an interpretive enterprise. Poetry as hermeneutics.

Hermeneutical Poetics and the Play of Metaphor

The distinction between exegetical and hermeneutical poetics can best be illustrated by contrasting the *Essay on Man* with a poem that rather famously foregrounds the interpretive process, "The Most of It," by Robert Frost:

> He thought he kept the universe alone;
> For all the voice in answer he could wake
> Was but the mocking echo of his own
> From some tree-hidden cliff across the lake.

Some morning from the boulder-broken beach
He would cry out on life, that what it wants
Is not its own love back in copy speech,
But counter-love, original response.
And nothing ever came of what he cried
Unless it was the embodiment that crashed
In the cliff's talus on the other side,
And then in the far-distant water splashed,
But after a time allowed for it to swim,
Instead of proving human when it neared
And someone else additional to him,
As a great buck it powerfully appeared,
Pushing the crumpled water up ahead,
And landed pouring like a waterfall,
And stumbled through the rocks with horny tread,
And forced the underbrush—and that was all.

(*A Witness Tree* 23)

When we begin to distinguish between subjective and objective experience, when we begin to question our ability to perceive reality independent of the shaping and distorting lenses of desire, we find ourselves in the realm of hermeneutics, at times confronted by the specter of solipsism. The fear of solipsism is stated in the first lines of this poem: "He thought he kept the universe alone;/For all the voice in answer he could wake/Was but the mocking echo of his own/From some tree-hidden cliff across the lake." The main, perhaps only, character of this hermeneutic narrative, alone and taunted by the echo of his desire, longs for the balm of "counter-love, original response."

But Frost offers little solace. As Guy Rotella has noted, Frost's "hesitant diction"—words like "thought," "some," and "Unless"—provides cold comfort to the poem's lonely character (85). Not only does he worry that the apparition of the "buck" may be a mere projection ("And nothing ever came of what he cried") but he is also unsure, once something appears, or seems to appear, what exactly he is witnessing. He strains to characterize this hypothetical Other. At first he can distinguish it only as an undistinguished "embodiment," but eventually it resolves into the form of a buck. Or does it? Even Rotella, who is extraordinarily attentive to Frost's strategies of ambiguity, accepts the buck as something near fact in this poem, noting only "the syntactical likelihood that if the buck embodies anything at all it embodies 'nothing'" (87). But the "buck" appears in the figure of a simile: "*As* a great buck it powerfully appeared" (emphasis mine). And while some of its behavior is definitive enough ("And stumbled through the rocks with horny tread, / And forced the underbrush"), the "buck's" landing, "pouring like a waterfall," is yet another simile, and an oddly cubist one at that, suggesting again the indeterminacy of perspective in this poem. Perhaps something real, something truly Other, does appear to the main character in this narrative, but it remains all appearance embodied in figures, "copy speech."

If there is consolation in "The Most of It" it is to be found only in the observation that whatever its form, the "embodiment" is not human: "Instead of proving human when it neared / And someone else additional to him, / As a great buck it powerfully appeared." This negative knowledge registers as surprise in the poem, suggesting the possibility, perhaps, of an "original response." The reason that the "buck" appears "powerfully" may be attributable to the shock of its nonhuman form rather than as simply the property of a mature male deer.

It is difficult to gauge the tone of the final, summarizing words in this poem ("and that was all"), but I am tempted to argue that they point to the significance of this negative knowledge; it may not be enough to satisfy our need for "counter-love," but at least it is something. Lowering one's sights, accepting in the startling presence of the nonhuman a modest and almost wholly attenuated victory over solipsism, may be what it means to make the most of our encounters with nonhuman nature.

In contrasting hermeneutical and exegetical poetics, I have implied, at least, that hermeneutics has superseded exegesis and may be somewhat synonymous with contemporary poetics (at least as practiced in countries with democratic political and aesthetic traditions). The problem with this implication is that it overstates both the mandate and the coherence of hermeneutical poetics. To understand sufficiently why this is the case, we need to trace the evolution of hermeneutical and exegetical poetics, an ambitious project the comprehensive fulfillment of which is beyond the scope of the present inquiry. We can, however, begin to sketch an outline of this critical history, a summary that may help explain why "contemporary nature poetry" is such a vexed, and vexing, enterprise.

Formally considered, an exegetical poetics depends upon a correspondence between reality, comprehension, and representation. Such a poetics lends itself to idealism, the correspondence among comprehension, representation, and a supermundane realm, as we see in the *Essay on Man*. Not only does Pope claim knowledge of a transcendental ideal in that poem, but, more important, it is the existence of the ideal, antecedent to his knowledge of it, that corroborates, and authorizes, his representation of it.

In terms of "correspondence," then, we see quickly that the differences between Pope's Neoclassicism and, say, Emerson's Romanticism is not very momentous. The form of the poetics is reproduced, only in Emerson's Romanticism does Nature occupy an intermediate position between poet and the supermundane ideal: "Every natural fact is a symbol of some spiritual fact," says Emerson, in a famous passage from "Nature." The task of the Romantic poet is to render the symbols of nature, and the poetic consciousness capable of recognizing them, in such a way so as to discern the Spirit inscribed therein. To be sure, learning to read the text of Nature adequately may require some reeducation, which is why Romantic poets tend to spend a great deal of time, in their poems and especially in their prose manifestos (for example, the many prefaces to the *Lyrical Ballads* and chapter 13 of the *Lyrical Ballads*), instructing us how to train our minds so that we, too, might develop the right kind of imaginative perception.

In symbolism we see yet another recapitulation of exegetical poetics. As an aspect of Romanticism, symbolist poets from Coleridge to Baudelaire to Crane preserve and exploit the correspondences between the material world and certain metaphysical realities. Even as symbolists abandoned the Romantic concern with Nature, and thus disengaged the symbol from the nonhuman, it still served to establish and reflect the correspondences between individual experience and spiritual, psychological, or even "sensual" realities. In this vein, while the poetry of, for example, Yeats, Poe, and Sandburg may be manifestly distinct, their poetics are remarkably similar.

It may be said that the development of a hermeneutical poetics occurs when we lose faith in the existence of a corroborating and authorizing agency, be it God or Truth or Mind or Matter, or when our ability to ascertain correspondences adequately is suspect. When the "transcendentalist" motion from the mundane and specific to the ideal and illimitable becomes, for one reason or another, significantly troubled, the ambition of poetry is correspondingly attenuated. Which might suggest that the development of a hermeneutical poetics is in fact contemporaneous with "modernity," if we identify modernity with post-Kantian, post-Darwinian, post-Nietzschean, post-Freudian struggles for and with meaning. If we consider the poetics of some of those most typically associated with modernism, however, our equation of modernity with hermeneutical poetics is quickly troubled.

Take Pound. The "processes" that Pound employs (collage, fragmentation, parataxis) are strategies in the pursuit of what is often called a verbal cubism, a poetic "mode" that ostensibly avoids exegesis. But as William Bevis, among others, has pointed out, the use of such devices in the name of "indeterminacy" does not necessarily indicate a shift in poetics:

> Early cubism in art and language (imagism) had some stylistic features we can depend on: hard, precise, delineated fragments. But philosophically—cubism could go either of two ways: the fragments could be seen as supporting relativity of point of view because in their contrary clues they thwart understanding and suggest process, the absence of tradition, the space between themselves as subject. On the other hand, the fragments could suggest a new idealism, made of hard facts, stasis, and theory—lines connecting the dots. (303)

Bevis argues that Pound ultimately embraces the second (exegetical) poetics, and for this reason he charges Pound with betraying the promise of modernism; failing in his attempt to invent "an impersonal geometry or to imitate a fragmented world," Pound succeeds only in creating "a new romanticism or neoclassicism under the guise of an avant-garde." Following Donald Davie, Bevis observes: "From the very beginning, Pound was a conservative imagist. . . . Collage was a way to be certain. Pound was one of those who, while leading the revolution, was also reacting against it" (303).[5]

From this perspective, the *Cantos* appear less audacious and revolutionary than Poundians like to admit. Bevis is unsparing: "The *Cantos* are not indeterminate. They are vision masquerading as collage. *The Four Zoas* cut up and pasted." While acknowledging that "the *Cantos* may be a mess and Pound may be right that they contain many wanderings and mistakes," Bevis insists, correctly I think, that "the goal that guides the form remains final, certain knowledge of history and culture." Bevis notes the significance of the fact that Pound's own "phrases for his project favor fixed nouns modified toward the universal and epiphanic: luminous details, radiant gists.

They exist beyond the perceiver, forever" (306). On this account, Pound and his arch-modernist kinsman, T. S. Eliot, may be said to profess the same exegetical creed: whereas Eliot ultimately shores up the fragments of history and culture against the rock of Christianity, Pound collects his own fragments and deploys them within the Poundian curriculum of right history, right economics, and right literary criticism: the ABCs of reading à la Pound.

But if we look beyond the usual modernist suspects, I think we can begin to discern the development of an authentic hermeneutical poetics in "modern" American poetry. Certainly the poetics of Emily Dickinson bears examination in this context, as does that of Gertrude Stein. (For example, we could ask to what extent is "Susie Asado" an attempt to represent, or avoid representing, the famous flamenco dancer of that name?) I believe, though, with Rotella, that it is in the work of such poets as Robert Frost, Wallace Stevens, Marianne Moore, and Elizabeth Bishop that we are able to observe a real departure from poetry as exegesis. Interestingly enough, all four of these poets are poets of nature, although in ways that invite us to reexamine how we conceive of the genre. Rotella argues that these poets

> continue and contest the American tradition of turning to nature in order to pose epistemological and aesthetic questions about how and how much we know about the power of art and artists to discover or create meaning and form. The tradition is a familiar one: it begins with confidence that nature is a book inscribed by God for men and women to read; it "ends" with the suspicion that nature's many texts are written by ourselves on a blank page or a palimpsest. The initial confidence was always uneasy; the recent suspicion is sometimes a source of delight. What began as a search for the meaning of God now questions the meaning of meaning. (ix)

If Rotella is right about these poets, then we have in their work an alternative to the "exegetical modernism" of Pound and his disciples, and the emergence of a "hermeneutical" nature poetry that continues to influence the way poets approach the nonhuman.

The bloodlines become tangled, however, in the confusion that attends critical discussion of modernism and postmodernism. If, for example, the "postmodern" can be summarized, in Lyotard's famous shorthand, as "incredulity toward metanarratives,"[6] Frost, Stevens, Moore, and Bishop may be said to practice a kind of postmodernism and are therefore, rather than Pound, the real progenitors of "postmodern" poetry.[7]

Of course, these four twentieth-century American poets were not the first to "turn to nature in order to pose epistemological and esthetic questions," an observation that should complicate this narrative, and deservedly so. It is clear, for example, that what makes the best Romantic poetry interesting is not its warmed-over Platonism but rather its *struggle* with idealism. When Wordsworth writes, in "Tintern Abbey":

> Therefore am I still
> A lover of the meadows and the woods,
> And mountains; and of all that we behold
> From this green earth; of all the mighty world
> Of eye, and ear,—both what they half create,
> And what perceive; well pleased to recognise
> In nature and the language of the sense
> The anchor of my purest thoughts, the nurse,
> The guide, the guardian of my heart, and soul
> Of all my moral being.
>
> (104)

he underscores, as in so many of his poems, the creative and redemptive power of the poetic imagination. But as many critics have noted, the tension between projection and perception in Romantic poetry, between a world half-created and half-perceived, is not always happily resolved, as it is in these lines. The darker moods of Romanticism speak to the intractable nature of the Romantic imagination. It is, in fact, a relatively short step from the comfort of "Tintern Abbey" to the terror of the young boater in book I of the *Prelude*. It is another short step, I would argue, to the hermeneutic distress of the central character of "The Most of It."

If the seeds that produced the most recent crop of "hermeneutical" poetry were sown by Romantic poets tormented by the problems attending imaginative vision, I think we do well to recognize the heirloom quality of such seeds. For it is the case that the questions concerning our ability to understand and represent reality, around which the Romantics and their successors dance, were posed by Greek intellectuals long before young Wordsworth was scared out of his wits in his little dinghy. (There are certainly non-Western roots for this concern with hermeneutics, but here I am limiting discussion to the Western canon.) I would like to suggest that the distinction made by "contemporary" poets, in practice or in theory, between exegetical and hermeneutical poetics represents, if not a footnote to Plato, then a series of footnotes to Protagoras, Gorgias, and Aristotle.

I have said that a hermeneutical poetics is made possible when we lose faith in the existence of a corroborating and authorizing agency or when our ability to ascertain correspondences is in doubt. Such a view reflects the consequences of a "Sophistic" critique of knowledge. The Sophists were speechwriters and teachers of oratory who were active in Athens in the fifth century B.C.E. One of them, Protagoras, challenged the availability of universal knowledge, maintaining that "truth" is ultimately inaccessible. His contemporary Gorgias held similar views and argued, furthermore, that opinion (*doxa*) is consequently the only guide to action.

Plato, of course, insisted that the Sophists were wrong, that Truth does exist, and that it is accessible through proper reasoning. He attacked the Sophists' art of rhetoric because it concerned itself with probabilities rather than certainties. Thus in the *Phaedrus*, Socrates assails the Sophists because

> They say that there is no need of treating these matters with such gravity and carrying them back so far to first principles with many words; for, as we said in the beginning of this discussion, he who is to be a competent rhetorician need have nothing at all to do, they say, with truth in considering things which are just or good, or men who are so, whether by nature or by education. For in the courts, they say, nobody cares for truth about these matters, but for that which is convincing; and that is probability, so that he who is to be an artist in speech must fix his attention upon probability. (272Eff)

Plato wanted to supplant the Sophists' misguided craft of rhetoric with a "legitimate" art: dialectic. For Plato, dialectic is a true art (*technē*) because it trades in ideal knowledge (*epistēmē*).[8]

Plato's most famous disciple, Aristotle, attempted a kind of compromise between the Sophistic and Platonic positions. His great contribution was to distinguish between realms of certain and probablistic knowledge and the arts proper to each. As Thomas Conley notes, Aristotle recognized that Plato's identification of genuine art (*technē*) exclusively with universal knowledge (*epistēmē*)

> conflated two different kinds of knowledge, and in doing so limited the range of intellectual activity that could legitimately be called a technē. One who claimed to be in possession of a technē did not have to have knowledge of universals, only of what is generally the case, "what happens for the most part." (14)

According to Aristotle, the art of dialectic consists of "demonstrations," or arguments, that proceed from premises (*protaseis*) based in truth (or "universal opinion," *epistēmē*), whereas the art of rhetoric consists of arguments that proceed from *doxa*, or particular opinion. (Aristotle also reserved a third category, "sophistic," for verbal play removed from argumentation, usually for questionable purposes.)

Insofar as an exegetical poetics springs from knowledge of truth, it is "epistemological," and therefore a kind of dialectical practice. And since a hermeneutical poetics springs from something less, or other, than certain knowledge, it is properly identified as a rhetorical practice, inasmuch as it retains an ambition toward some kind of knowledge. Shunning any such ambition, a hermeneutical poetics shades from rhetoric toward the sheerly Sophistic.

From the perspective of exegetical poetics, hermeneutical poetics looks like an unnecessary compromise or, worse, a fraud: if certain knowledge is available, to dabble in mere probabilities, or to raise questions about our ability to ascertain the truth, seems disingenuous and Sophistical. On the other hand, from the perspective of hermeneutical poetics, exegetical poetics reflects unrealistic ambitions or worse: to lay claim to the truth seems arrogant and potentially dangerous.

For Robert Frost, and for other poets who embrace a hermeneutical poetics, to think that poets have a choice between exegetical and hermeneutical poetics is to misunderstand poetry itself. Frost argues that the metaphorical basis of poetry implies an essential hermeneutical poetics. To understand this metaphorical basis is, in Frost's words, to get "educated by poetry." "Education by poetry," he maintains, "is education by metaphor" ("Education" 35).

According to Frost, poetry discloses the strengths, and weaknesses, of metaphor. The *power* of poetry lies primarily in metaphor's ability to establish a sense of meaningful relationship: "Poetry begins in trivial metaphors, pretty metaphors, 'grace' metaphors, and goes on to the profoundest thinking that we have. Poetry [through metaphor] provides the one permissible way of saying one thing and meaning another" (36). But this power is limited by the fact that "All metaphor breaks down somewhere" (41), that is, a metaphor that holds in one realm of experience may not serve in another, or time may rob metaphor of its salience. While it is true that metaphors may have such a reach that, over time, they take on the aura of truths, their status qua metaphor foreshadows their potential for obsolescence.

To be truly educated by poetry, then, is to come to terms with both aspects of metaphor. Frost essays a metaphor of cohabitation to define this process:

> That is the beauty of it. It is touch and go with the metaphor, and until you have lived with it long enough you don't know when it is going. You don't know how much you can get out of it and when it will cease to yield. It is a very living thing. It is as life itself. (41)

Learning to live with metaphor means becoming comfortable with its mutable disposition. Lacking such "domestic sympathy," one is left in the figurative lurch:

> What I am pointing out is that unless you are at home in the metaphor, unless you have had your proper poetical education in the metaphor, you are not safe anywhere. Because you are not at ease with figurative values: you don't know the metaphor in its strengths and its weakness. You don't know how far you may expect to ride it and when it may break down with you. (39)

Here, metaphor as housemate is transformed into metaphor as vehicle, or rather, metaphor as saddle animal ("It is a very living thing"). Learning how to be "at ease with figurative values," and how to exercise metaphor short of exhaustion, becomes the goal of education by poetry.

Most significantly, if one is "at ease with figurative values," one is free to offer metaphor, says Frost, as a "momentary stay against confusion" (or in Stevens's terminology, as a "fiction") instead of as conclusion, or conclusive fact ("Figure" 18). Further, one learns to treat all metaphor, not just one's own, with discretion. "I do not think anybody ever knows the discreet use of metaphor, his own and other people's, the discreet handling of metaphor, unless he has been properly educated in poetry" ("Education" 36). Education by poetry thus entails both a *poetics*, circumscribing how one should regard the product of one's own invention, and an *ethic* of reading, in that we are enjoined to handle the metaphors offered by others with some care.

How, then, do we tell the difference between the discreet and the indiscreet handling of metaphor, between poetry offered "as if" true and poetry offered as truth? In one sense, we simply cannot. Consider Carol Frost's poem "Sexual Jealousy":

> Think of the queen mole who is unequivocal,
> exuding a scent to keep the other females neuter
> and bringing forth the colony's only babies, hairless and pink in the dark
> of her tunneled chamber. She may chew a pale something, a root,
> find it tasteless, drop it for the dreary others to take away, then demand
> more; she must suckle the young. Of course
> they all hate her and are jealous of the attention given her
> by her six bedmates. In their mutual dream she is dead and her urine
> no longer arrests their maturing. As irises infallibly unfold,
> one of their own will feel her sex grow quickest and greatest. As they dig
> together, their snouts full of soil, they hope this and are ruthless
> in their waiting.
>
> (21)

Does the poet here really think she knows moles well enough to characterize their dreams, their emotions, their social and biological organization? Nothing in the poem would suggest her knowledge of moles is merely suggestive or provisional. And the business concerning the prophylactic effect of mole urine smacks of ecological authenticity. But who is to say that the poet has *not* received a proper education by poetry and has accordingly offered this glimpse into the inner lives of moles "as if" it were true? Are we not being indiscreet readers by questioning Carol Frost's representational ambitions in this poem?

For that matter, how do we know that Pope, ever vigilant against the excesses of human rationality, was not himself educated by poetry? If we could question him, wouldn't he say that, of course, the Great Chain of Being is merely a useful (and well-worn) metaphor, that his vision of the cosmos, while obviously grand, is merely one man's view, offered for our delight and instruction, and that we are wrong (and mean-spirited) to charge him with "epistemology," or truth telling?

My point here is that it may be difficult, if not impossible, to distinguish between poetry that derives from an exegetical poetics and poetry that derives from a hermeneutical poetics. To do so we need to be able to ascertain the level of "conviction" a poet brings to his or her vision. Perhaps Pope's rhetoric of "Order," his invocation of "Heaven's design," is enough to give us pause. Without such explicit "epistemological signaling," however, we need to carefully examine our reasons for identifying the metaphorical indiscretions of others lest we commit an indiscretion ourselves, mistaking the nightingale for the bird of paradise, as it were. It is sobering, and instructive, to consider to what extent contemporary literary criticism is guilty of such indiscretion.[9]

As exegesis gives way to hermeneutics, such "epistemological signaling" becomes the exception that proves the rule. Under the sign of rhetoric, poets are much more likely to announce the contingency of their vision than its timeless validity. The strategies for doing this are many; they are in fact the catalog of strategies that distinguishes modern and postmodern poetics. These include, in the first place, making room for more than one perspective in a poem: "dialogism" by way of dramatic dialogue and collage.[10] A second strategy involves the use of rhetorical structures such as antithesis, parataxis, and ellipsis to accentuate the argumentative (rhetorical) nature of poetry's claim to knowledge. Third, the contingency of vision can be explicitly acknowledged by becoming the *subject* of poetry, as in "The Most of It," by Robert Frost.

What all these strategies have in common is that they bracket the poet's commitment to the vision being offered in his or her poem, thus ensuring that meaning is kept in play, to one extent or another. Although metaphors can and do "break down," during their effective lifetimes they are capable of becoming rigid structures (or perhaps it is our relationship to them that becomes unyielding), thereby arresting the potential for alternate perspective. The tendency toward such rigidity, the inclination toward certainty, risks the forfeiture of a poetic practice premised on a hermeneutical poetics. "Progress is not the aim," says Frost, "but circulation" (Rotella 61).

In his poem "Birches," Frost enacts the necessary motion of metaphor. He also presents a character who is distinctly "at ease with figurative values," master of his medium:

> Some boy too far from town to learn baseball,
> Whose only play was what he found himself,
> Summer or winter, and could play alone.
> One by one he subdued his father's trees
> By riding them down over and over again
> Until he took the stiffness out of them,
> And not one but hung limp, not one was left
> For him to conquer. He learned all there was
> To learn about not launching out too soon
> And so not carrying the tree away
> Clear to the ground. He always kept his poise
> To the top branches, climbing carefully
> With the same pains you use to fill a cup
> Up to the brim, and even above the brim.
> Then he flung outward, feet first, with a swish,
> Kicking his way down through the air to the ground.
>
> (*Mountain Interval* 37–40)

Clearly the boy in this poem knows how to get the most mileage out of a metaphor. He knows how to groom each one so that it is neither too stiff nor too supple, knows how to ride a metaphor so that it neither flings him off into transcendental excess nor dashes him, in its "decline," to the very material, and unforgiving, ground. As a metaphor for metaphor, the birch tree mediates between extremes. And as a figure representing Frost's poetic ideal, the boy in this poem, proving that discretion is the better part of valor, knows enough to want to avoid going to extremes.

The speaker in the poem recognizes in the boy Frost's ideal and aspires to it:

> So was I once myself a swinger of birches.
> And so I dream of going back to be.
> It's when I'm weary of considerations,
> And life is too much like a pathless wood
> Where your face burns and tickles with the cobwebs
> Broken across it, and one eye is weeping
> From a twig's having lashed across it open.
> I'd like to get away from earth awhile
> And then come back to it and begin over.
> May no fate willfully misunderstand me
> And half grant what I wish and snatch me away
> Not to return. Earth's the right place for love:
> I don't know where it's likely to go better.

Here the speaker describes, in poignant detail, the two poles between which the "swinger of birches" hopes to oscillate. On the one hand are the contingencies of mundane existence that, not surprisingly, literally interfere with one's ability to envision different metaphors, alternative possibilities: the twig-lashed eye. On the other hand is the realm of transcendental experience, which, in the logic of the poem, and as a figure for the dissolution of a hermeneutical poetics into an exegetical poetics, argues against return to the play of meaning.

Avoiding either extreme, the speaker settles for the "momentary stay" and the opportunity to take another ride offered by the play of metaphor within a hermeneutical poetics.

We might be right, though, to wonder if Frost is perhaps a little too self-satisfied with the hermeneutical regime presented in "Birches." The boy's willful cockiness contributes a note of smugness to the scene, even as the speaker articulates the dangers of swinging that a more seasoned perspective admits. We note, too, that the boy's play is hardly a perpetual motion, that in the end he seems to have exhausted all the possibilities that "his father's trees" seem to offer: "And not one but hung limp, not one was left/For him to conquer."

If we regard the poem in its entirety (for I have snuck in only the idyllic parts), we see that Frost's stance regarding the supposed metaphoric mastery of the young boy, and the more humble, weather-beaten skill of the older speaker, is much more complex than I have so far acknowledged. Consider the beginning of the poem, previously omitted:

> When I see birches bend to left and right
> Across the lines of straighter darker trees,
> I like to think some boy's been swinging them.
> But swinging doesn't bend them down to stay
> As ice storms do. Often you must have seen them
> Loaded with ice a sunny winter morning
> After a rain. They click upon themselves
> As the breeze rises, and turn many-colored
> As the stir cracks and crazes their enamel.
> Soon the sun's warmth makes them shed crystal shells
> Shattering and avalanching on the snow crust—
> Such heaps of broken glass to sweep away
> You'd think the inner dome of heaven had fallen.
> They are dragged to the withered bracken by the load,
> And they seem not to break; though once they are bowed
> So low for long, they never right themselves:
> You may see their trunks arching in the woods

> Years afterwards, trailing their leaves on the ground
> Like girls on hands and knees that throw their hair
> Before them over their heads to dry in the sun.
> But I was going to say when Truth broke in
> With all her matter of fact about the ice storm,
> I should prefer to have some boy bend them
> As he went out and in to fetch the cows—
> Some boy too far from town [. . .]

The speaker concedes that the mastery that the boy seems to exhibit in the poem is, in point of fact, a fantasy, something he would "prefer." But even though he'd "like to think" that some boy is responsible for bending the trees, he recognizes the fact of the matter, that an ice storm is usually to blame. Having bowed to the force of Nature, the speaker admits the Truth.

Not that the Truth arrests the motion of metaphor in "Birches." It may put a temporary halt to the proliferation of figurative language in the poem (the figures of the swinging boy, the "dome of heaven" and the "girls on hands and knees that throw their hair/Before them over their heads to dry in the sun"), but the poem quickly moves on to introduce Frost's poetic ideal and back to the conceit of the boy swinging trees so well and so hard that they remain arched, "conquered." Modulating again, the speaker reenters the poem, dreaming of "going back" to his younger self but qualifying youthful zeal with the wisdom that age and suffering permit. At the end of this ride, the speaker of the poem, and perhaps the reader, may have encountered Truth, may have discovered "the right place for love," but he and we are also somewhat chastened by the experience.

If "Birches" may be said to enact the ideal it characterizes, it is clear that the ideal suffers a bit in the process. Consider, too, where the poem puts us down as it concludes:

> I'd like to go by climbing a birch tree,
> And climb black branches up a snow-white trunk

> *Toward* heaven, till the tree could bear no more,
> But dipped its top and set me down again.
> That would be good both going and coming back.
> One could do worse than be a swinger of birches.

Here the speaker counts on the strength of the birch, of metaphor, to support his desire to transcend the weariness of "considerations," to rescue him from "the pathless wood." But the speaker also counts on the limitations of metaphor to return him to earth, however pathless, and to the love that life on earth affords, even if there might be better places for it, as the speaker intimates. Both actions are good, both actions are necessary. "One could do worse than be a swinger of birches": yes, obviously. One can freeze in the rarefied air of truth, one can stumble aimlessly *per una selva oscura*. This final line of "Birches" is either terribly understated or terribly straightforward. I'd like to think it is both.

There is one further way in which Frost enacts the necessary metaphoric circulation that a hermeneutical poetics necessitates even as he presents his poetic ideal. We have seen how Frost resists "idealizing" his ideal by refusing to allow it free reign. Frost also restrains whatever momentum toward the ideal remains at the end of "Birches" through the "contradiction" of other poems, such as "In a Glass of Cider":

> It seemed I was a mite of sediment
> That waited for the bottom to ferment
> So I could catch a bubble in ascent.
> I rode up on one till the bubble burst,
> And when that left me to sink back reversed
> I was no worse off than I was at first.
> I'd catch another bubble if I waited.
> The thing was to get now and then elated.
>
> (*In the Clearing* 94)

Here Frost mocks the activity he ennobles in "Birches." The master metaphorician in this poem is a mere mite riding bubbles, getting "now and then elated." The tone of the poem, the banal figure of a glass of cider, both serve to parody Frost's poetic ideal. What might have been seen as the ecstatic liberty of the swinger of birches becomes the ludicrous vacillations of a glass-bound mite. By parodying his own poetic ideal, Frost complicates significantly the authority that we might want to ascribe to hermeneutical poetics. In so doing, Frost paradoxically reaffirms the value of that ideal.

Pragmatism and Environmental Poetics

But what does "Birches" have to say about the woods that surrounded Frost's farm in Derry, New Hampshire? (Or for that matter, what does "In a Glass of Cider" tell us about making, or drinking, that lovely beverage?) Before we miss entirely the forest for the trees, I'd like, in the balance of this chapter, to address the relationship between hermeneutical poetics and environmental poetry. I want to argue that a poetry of the environment that is grounded in a hermeneutical poetics is capable of reinforcing ecocentric values as it satisfies the very real need for, in Buell's words, "better ways of imaging nature and humanity's relation to it."

As I alluded to earlier, Rotella finds in the poetry of Frost, Stevens, Moore, and Bishop the emergence of what he calls an "epistemological nature poetry" (13), but which I would prefer to term "hermeneutical environmental poetry" for reasons that I hope are clear by now. According to Rotella, these poets

> turn to nature in order to pose epistemological and esthetic questions. Each suspects that all readings of transcendence, whether based on the Word or the natural world, are humanly inscribed, and that

> poetry and the poet are therefore radically limited in their capacity to know and to create. Yet each also continues the effort to discover or make meaningful patterns of order. Furthermore, each poet engages in that effort while simultaneously challenging the authority of every system of knowledge and of every work of art—including his or her own. All four poets affirm that the attempt to find or invent meaning is a vital and definitive human act (they are, at least to that degree, essentialists), yet each insists that the results of such attempts are at worst destructive frauds and at best conditional or "fictive" consolations, not redemptive truths. Each believes that if we are to live felicitous lives we require the provisional satisfactions that art and other cultural acts and structures provide, yet each remains subversively alert to the exclusion and oppression that occur when the provisional is taken as absolute and authoritative and is reified by power. (xi–xii)

If we are looking to poetry, and to poets, for the figures with which we might redeem a badly fractured environment and which would help us define our proper, if not original, relationship to the world, these poets, and poetry that embraces a similar poetics, would seem a dubious choice. For this is a poetry that is preeminently self-conscious about its own rhetoricity and that embraces irony as the best remedy for transcendental zeal.

I think, though, that we need to reconsider the aim of hermeneutical poetics. It is probably the case that most poets who adopt a hermeneutical poetics do so to be loyal to metaphor. In other words, one puts such a poetics into practice because it is the truest way for one to be with meaning, even if truth has little to do with it. But there is also a *social* dimension to the practice of hermeneutical poetics. One uses metaphor with discretion, in the sense Frost gives the term, to create room for other perspectives in the discourse. This is the *democratic* and ultimately *pragmatic* aspect of hermeneutical poetics. As Richard Rorty reminds us, while pragmatism is certainly the name of the "philosophy" championed by Peirce, James, Dewey, and their intellectual descendants, it does not find its basis in "purely philosophical principles." Rorty makes the important point that pragmatism, as a philosophy, is merely a philosophical rationale for certain *political* commitments. He heeds Dewey in identifying pragmatism as "a philosophy tailored to the needs of political liberalism, a way of making political liberalism look good to persons with philosophical tastes" (211).

If an ecocentric environmental ethic is premised on the extension of moral considerability to nonhuman beings, we need to examine just how such consideration is to be tendered. One way is to put the strength of metaphor to work, to use it as a vehicle for presenting the interests of the nonhuman within our discourse. But if we come to question the poet's ability to comprehend and to represent these interests, I would contend that the practice of a pragmatic hermeneutical poetics answers an ethical, if not political, mandate by simultaneously risking meaning through the offices of metaphor and insisting upon its conditional character. Even when our search for more responsible representations of the nonhuman is motivated sheerly by our love of nature, perhaps *because* it is inspired by love, it ought to be tempered by discursive discretion, "enthusiasm tamed by metaphor" (R. Frost, "Education," 36).

I believe that a number of contemporary poets have embraced a pragmatic environmental poetics that negotiates both their love of nature and their sense of discursive discretion. Working within the tradition of Frost, Stevens, Moore, and Bishop, and influenced by the discourses of ecology, these poets are exploring poetry's role in reconceptualizing our relationship to the natural world. One of the best is A. R. Ammons, a poet who came to environmental concerns well before environmentalism emerged as a popular preoccupation. By way of illustrating the potential for a pragmatic environmental poetics, I would like to turn in the final section to Ammons's poem

"Corsons Inlet." The poem will be useful for many reasons, not the least of which is because it serves as a meditation on both nature and nature writing.

Pragmatic Environmental Poetics in "Corsons Inlet"

> I went for a walk over the dunes again this morning
> to the sea,
> then turned right along
>   the surf
>   rounded a naked headland
>   and returned
>
>   along the inlet shore:
>
> it was muggy sunny, the wind from the sea steady and high,
> crisp in the running sand,
>   some breakthroughs of sun
>   but after a bit
>
> continuous overcast:

"Corsons Inlet" begins with a walk, a familiar one, along the margin of land and sea. The poem's line breaks recall the flux of the waves and weather, and of Ammons's peripatetic musings. He turns to contemplate the ebb and flow of his environment and of his mind:

> the walk liberating, I was released from forms,
> from the perpendiculars,
>   straight lines, blocks, boxes, binds
> of thought
> into the hues, shadings, rises, flowing bends and blends
>   of sight:

I allow myself eddies of meaning:
yield to a direction of significance
running
like a stream through the geography of my work:
you can find
in my sayings
swerves of action
like the inlet's cutting edge:
there are dunes of motion,
organizations of grass, white sandy paths of remembrance
in the overall wandering of mirroring mind:

The interplay of mind and mutable nature transforms the quality of consciousness. Ammons distinguishes "thought" (the ostensibly rigid "forms" of cognitive constructs, or precepts) from "sight" (the awareness of supple percepts that flow from immediate experience). "Liberated" from premeditated structure, Ammons returns to form, but in a way that reveals a pragmatic sensibility. "I allow myself eddies of meaning:/yield to a direction of significance." The figures of his thought are now provisional precipitants in a field that eludes definition:

but Overall is beyond me: is the sum of these events
I cannot draw, the ledger I cannot keep, the accounting
beyond the account:

in nature there are few sharp lines: there are areas of
primrose
more or less dispersed;
disorderly orders of bayberry; between the rows
of dunes,
irregular swamps of reeds,
though not reeds alone, but grass, bayberry, yarrow, all . . .
predominantly reeds:

> I have reached no conclusions, have erected no boundaries,
> shutting out and shutting in, separating inside
> from outside: I have
> drawn no lines:
> as
>
> manifold events of sand
> change the dune's shape that will not be the same shape
> tomorrow,
>
> so I am willing to go along, to accept
> the becoming
> thought, to stake off no beginnings or ends, establish
> no walls:
>
> by transitions the land falls from grassy dunes to creek
> to undercreek: but there are no lines, though
> change in that transition is clear
> as any sharpness: but "sharpness" spread out,
> allowed to occur over a wider range
> than mental lines can keep:

What emerges from this shift in consciousness, or attitude, is an environmental poetics that is responsive to the ontological autonomy of a world in flux. As there are "few sharp lines" in nature, Ammons declares that he is "willing to go along, to accept/the becoming/ thought," drawing lines that anticipate erasure, figures that predict mutation. His "mirroring mind" reflects the fluctuating play of an interanimated and not wholly discernible environment:

> the moon was full last night: today, low tide was low:
> black shoals of mussels exposed to the risk
> of air
> and, earlier, of sun,
>
> waved in and out with the waterline, waterline inexact,
> caught always in the event of change:

a young mottled gull stood free on the shoals
and ate
to vomiting: another gull, squawking possession, cracked a crab,
picked out the entrails, swallowed the soft-shelled legs, a ruddy
turnstone running in to snatch leftover bits:

risk is full: every living thing in
siege: the demand is life, to keep life: the small
white blacklegged egret, how beautiful, quietly stalks and spears
the shallows, darts to shore
to stab—what? I couldn't
see against the black mudflats—a frightened
fiddler crab?

the news to my left over the dunes and
reeds and bayberry clumps was
fall: thousands of tree swallows
gathering for flight:
an order held
in constant change: a congregation
rich with entropy: nevertheless, separable, noticeable
as one event,
not chaos: preparations for
flight from winter,
cheet, cheet, cheet, cheet, wings rifling the green clumps,
beaks
at the bayberries
a perception full of wind, flight, curve,
sound:
the possibility of rule as the sum of rulelessness:
the "field" of action
with moving, incalculable center:

Faced with the unruly motion and interpenetrating sprawl of the natural world, Ammons works toward an approach to nature, and to its representation, that acknowledges that any delineation of the environment implies a necessary imposition of order. It is in this sense that I believe Ammons's poetics reinforces an ecocentric ethic. By recognizing the vicissitudes of representation, Ammons shows respect for the ontological autonomy of the nonhuman, an essential aspect of an environmental ethic that seeks to decenter human perspective and deprivilege human experience. What remains is the trace of perception, a makeshift understanding that requires revision:

> in the smaller view, order tight with shape:
> blue tiny flowers on a leafless weed: carapace of crab:
> snail shell:
>   pulsations of order
>   in the bellies of minnows: orders swallowed,
> broken down, transferred through membranes
> to strengthen larger orders: but in the large view, no
> lines or changeless shapes: the working in and out, together
>   and against, of millions of events: this,
>   so that I make
>   no form of
>   formlessness:
>
> orders as summaries, as outcomes of actions override
> or in some way result, not predictably (seeing me gain
> the top of a dune,
> the swallows
> could take flight—some other fields of bayberry
>   could enter fall
>   berryless) and there is serenity:
>
>   no arranged terror: no forcing of image, plan,
> or thought:
> no propaganda, no humbling of reality to precept:
>
> terror pervades but is not arranged, all possibilities
> of escape open: no route shut, except in
>   the sudden loss of all routes:

> I see narrow orders, limited tightness, but will
> not run to that easy victory:
> still around the looser, wider forces work:
> I will try
> to fasten into order enlarging grasps of disorder, widening
> scope, but enjoying the freedom that
> Scope eludes my grasp, that there is no finality of vision,
> that I have perceived nothing completely,
> that tomorrow a new walk is a new walk.
>
> (5–8)

Environmental ethics imply an environmental poetics that is pragmatic in its engagement of the world. Such a poetics makes room for nonhuman alterity as it compensates for the vicissitudes of symbolic action. It is successful to the extent that it is responsive to both. The best environmental poetry thus reorients our relationship to nature and to language.

If "Corsons Inlet" represents the possibility of a productive and responsible environmental poetic, it also invokes the essential dilemma of symbolic action. For Ammons may proclaim, in good conscience, that "I have drawn no lines," but his lines of verse testify otherwise. And though he has vowed "to stake off no beginnings or ends," "Corsons Inlet" begins and ends like any other poem. Its greatest virtue, as I have tried to suggest in this chapter, is that it admits "no finality of vision" as it negotiates, and renegotiates, the contours of a world that is both perspicuous and ineffable. But as the product of epistemological and aesthetic judgments, "Corsons Inlet" also cannot escape the "humbling of reality to precept." In the final chapter, we will consider a refinement of the environmental poetics outlined here, one that confronts the dilemma of symbolic action more directly.

May we give true voice
To the statements of Thy creatures.
May our spoken words speak for them,
With accuracy,
That we know precisely their rejoinders
To our utterances,
And so may correct our utterances
In the light of those rejoinders.

—KENNETH BURKE,
"Dialectician's Hymn"

CHAPTER 5

Skeptical Environmental Poetics

Symbolic Action and Linguistic Skepticism

In his poem "Two Look at Two," Robert Frost describes an encounter between two hikers and a pair of deer on a darkening mountainside:

> Love and forgetting might have carried them
> A little further up the mountainside
> With night so near, but not much further up.
> They must have halted soon in any case
> With thoughts of the path back, how rough it was
> With rock and washout, and unsafe in darkness;
> When they were halted by a tumbled wall
> With barbed-wire binding. They stood facing this,

Spending what onward impulse they still had
In one last look the way they must not go,
On up the failing path, where, if a stone
Or earthslide moved at night, it moved itself;
No footstep moved it. "This is all," they sighed,
"Good-night to woods." But not so; there was more.
A doe from round a spruce stood looking at them
Across the wall, as near the wall as they.
She saw them in their field, they her in hers.
The difficulty of seeing what stood still,
Like some up-ended boulder split in two,
Was in her clouded eyes: they saw no fear there.
She seemed to think that, two thus, they were safe.
Then, as if they were something that, though strange,
She could not trouble her mind with too long,
She sighed and passed unscared along the wall.
"*This*, then, is all. What more is there to ask?"
But no, not yet. A snort to bid them wait.
A buck from round the spruce stood looking at them
Across the wall, as near the wall as they.
This was an antlered buck of lusty nostril,
Not the same doe come back into her place.
He viewed them quizzically with jerks of head,
As if to ask, "Why don't you make some motion?
Or give some sign of life? Because you can't.
I doubt if you're as living as you look."
Thus till he had them almost feeling dared
To stretch a proffering hand—and a spell-breaking.
Then he too passed unscared along the wall.
Two had seen two, whichever side you spoke from.
"This *must* be all." It was all. Still they stood,
A great wave from it going over them,
As if the earth in one unlooked-for favor
Had made them certain earth returned their love.

(*New Hampshire* 95–96)

Late in the day, the hikers arrest their excursion up the mountain, in part due to fatigue, in part due to the hour and their sense of the long and rough trip back. Their stopping place is one of those zones that Frost so often explored: the margin between human cultivation and something wilder, something different. It is delineated by "a tumbled wall / With barbed-wire binding," the kind of barrier one often comes across in the mountains of the northeastern United States, evidence of abandoned ambitions to live high up in stony woods.

"Love and forgetting might have carried them / A little further up the mountainside / With night so near, but not much further up." Beyond the wall, up the "failing path," is a region unfrequented by human traffic, "where, if a stone/Or earthslide moved at night, it moved itself;/No footstep moved it." Checked by their fatigue and the coming nightfall, the hikers acknowledge the terminus of their effort, albeit with some reluctance. "'This is all,' they sighed, 'Good-night to woods.'"

"But not so," the speaker of the poem attests; "there was more." It is at this moment, the instant of their abandoning the effort to push on, that the hikers are treated to a kind of visitation. The something "more" takes the form of a doe who, "from round a spruce stood looking at them/Across the wall, as near the wall as they." What transpires then is a moment of real intimacy in which the hikers and the doe are reflected in each other's sight, though they remain on their respective sides of the wall: "She saw them in their field, they her in hers."

The moment of intimacy passes as the doe sighs (echoing the hikers' sighs) and moves along, "unscared." The hikers, seemingly moved by the surprise encounter, conclude that they have experienced all they are likely to experience: "'*This*, then, is all. What more is there to ask?'" In answer to their rhetorical question, the speaker again corrects their deduction, promising still more: "But no, not yet." This time, something "more" takes the form of "an antlered buck of lusty nostril":

> He viewed them quizzically with jerks of head,
> As if to ask, "Why don't you make some motion?
> Or give some sign of life? Because you can't.
> I doubt if you're as living as you look."

Significantly, I think, both visitations, both moments of intimacy, are made possible by the utter stillness of the hikers. The doe approaches because the hikers stand motionless:

> The difficulty of seeing what stood still,
> Like some up-ended boulder split in two,
> Was in her clouded eyes: they saw no fear there.
> She seemed to think that, two thus, they were safe.

The buck, who appears to have a less "clouded" view of the hikers, confronts them more directly, snorting and shaking his head, very nearly taunting them into action: "Thus till he had them almost feeling dared/To stretch a proffering hand—and a spell-breaking." But the hikers remain immobile, refusing to break the spell: "Then he too passed unscared along the wall."

The poem concludes with some of the most decidedly heartening lines that Frost ever offered:

> Two had seen two, whichever side you spoke from.
> "This *must* be all." It was all. Still they stood,
> A great wave from it going over them,
> As if the earth in one unlooked-for favor
> Had made them certain earth returned their love.

Which is not to say that the consolation extended in these lines is completely free from Frost's typical qualification. The poem does not simply assert the earth's gift as fact, nor their understanding of it as certain; these characterizations are presented "as if" true. But unlike similar moments in other poems in which Frost radically attenuates the kinds of solace we might hope for, the hikers' experience seems almost altogether genuine, the wave real, the gift authentic, their appreciation substantial.

In this final chapter I would like to take this moment in "Two Look at Two" as paradigmatic of our encounter with the nonhuman and use it to explore further questions of knowledge and ethics as they pertain to environmental writing in general and environmental poetry in particular. I would like to begin by considering what the humans bring to the tumbled wall and what we might say about the respective "fields" from which the hikers and the deer regard one another.

In an important and fundamental sense, Frost's division of the two "fields" is artificial. Both the deer and the humans share a common material reality; in ecological terms, they are both members of ecosystems that sustain their existence. On this level, the encounter, which is the occasion for "Two Look at Two," is merely a meeting between two kinds of animals, different in form and motivation, perhaps, but ultimately similar in terms of their physiological situation.

Taking their common material condition as given, I would like to bring into focus a difference that may be said to obtain between the animals who meet at Frost's tumbled wall, a difference that serves to distinguish their respective domains even as it is grounded in an undifferentiated sphere of existence. However we might like to characterize the human animal, its most pronounced attribute is its proclivity to produce and manipulate symbols. As Kenneth Burke has argued, the propensity for symbol use can be seen as *the* defining property of the human species: "Man is the symbol-using animal" (*Language* 3). Here is Burke's whole formula:

> Man is
> the symbol-using (symbol-making, symbol-misusing) animal
> inventor of the negative (or moralized by the negative)

separated from his natural condition by instruments of his own making
goaded by the spirit of hierarchy (or moved by the sense of order)
and rotten with perfection.

(16)

According to Burke, humans use symbols to further a range of motives running the gamut of human interests and desires. Because symbol use requires a certain level of cooperation, and corresponds with a rather high degree of self-consciousness (sufficient to produce, for instance, the idea of the Self, and of the Other), it represents a kind of *action* as opposed to the mere *motion* of things. As we noted in chapter 2, for this reason Burke distinguishes the realm of *symbolic action* from the realm of *nonsymbolic motion*, the strictly material or physiological realm of existence.[1]

Inasmuch as symbol use is the distinguishing characteristic of the human species, it is an activity of which humans are obviously capable and for which we seem to have a special affinity. It may be simply that, as Burke notes, "We symbolize because we *like* to symbolize" (29). We also symbolize, I would add, because to a great extent we cannot seem to avoid it.

Whether we view our propensity for symbolic action as a talent or a compulsion, our reliance on it generates a unique set of consequences for the human species, consequences that condition our approach to our environment. The first consequence of symbolic action is that humans have the ability to generate symbols with the potential to influence how we live in the world. These symbols (and symbolic regimes) may align themselves with our needs as physiological beings, as when we win our bread through the work we do, work that in itself may have nothing to do with procuring food. Alternatively, the symbols we generate may run counter to our needs as physiological organisms, as when, in the name of "progress" or "patriotism" or some such, we build up huge concentrations of toxic and radioactive matter with the potential to degrade or destroy entirely the material basis for our existence.

In previous chapters I examined some of the symbols and symbol systems that have been deployed as the human species attempts to redefine its relationship to the nonhuman. These include especially the symbols generated by ecological discourse: ecology as an overarching pattern of ontological and ethical organization, the nonhuman speaking subject, alinguistic agency, and so forth. As Burke suggests, these attempts to arrive at a better relationship to the world through symbolic action constitute a uniquely human enterprise. By cooperating through language in our search for a better relationship to the nonhuman realm, we reveal our own special nature.

If our habit of symbolic action affords us the opportunity to exploit language in the pursuit of a new environmental ethic, it also dictates that we suffer the handicaps that symbolic action necessarily entails. The first of these handicaps derives from the semiotic structure of the symbol, the soi-disant "split signifier." As Burke points out, the split signifier creates an essential disjunction between *res* and *verba*, "things and the words for things":

> Language referring to the realm of the nonverbal is necessarily talk about things in terms of what they are not—and in this sense we start out beset by a paradox. Such language is but a set of labels, signs for helping us find our way about. Indeed, they can even be so useful that they help us to invent ingenious ways of threatening to destroy ourselves. But even accuracy of this powerful sort does not get around the fact that such terms are sheer emptiness, as compared with the substance of the things they name. (5)

Even if, as Burke points out, our symbols prove to be useful tools for "negotiating" the world, the structure of the split signifier raises the possibility, at least, that our sense of reality corresponds with the symbols at hand rather than with nonsymbolic "substances." On this point Burke asks:

> The "symbol-using animal," yes, obviously. But can we bring ourselves to realize just what that formula implies, just how overwhelmingly much of what we mean by "reality" has been built up for us through nothing but our symbol-systems? (5)

In a sense, Burke spent the better part of the twentieth century answering this question. By helping us understand the full implications of symbolic action, and especially the ways in which we "confuse" (for good or ill) the symbolic and the nonsymbolic, Burke provides us with a productive standpoint from which to consider the horizon of our symbolic understanding of the world. I will consider what may lie over that horizon in a moment.

The second handicap entailed by symbolic action stems from the way in which symbols tend to focus our perception. Burke refers to the more or less obvious fact that "any nomenclature necessarily directs the attention into some channels rather than others." By directing our attention, symbols inevitably turn us away from certain aspects of reality as they turn us toward others. They thus function as what Burke calls "terministic screens." "Even if a given terminology is a *reflection* of reality," says Burke, "by its very nature as a terminology it must be a *selection* of reality; and to this extent it must function also as a *deflection* of reality" (45). When we consider the fact that symbols are ultimately not things, and that they inevitably direct our attention away from facets of our world, I think we must agree with Burke that, to some degree at least (and therein lies the rub), we are separated from our "natural condition" by these "instruments of [our] own making."

A third handicap entailed by symbolic action originates in what Burke calls the "entelechial principle." As I noted in chapter 2, Burke uses the term "entelechy" to describe the "inertia" that terms seem to possess, which necessarily involves symbolic action in the (abstracted or material) tragedy of "purification" and concomitant "scapegoating."

Given these significant handicaps, what kind of environmental poetry is possible? We might be inclined to conclude that language is an insuperable barrier capable only of separating us from the natural world. But such a conclusion overemphasizes the ways in which language estranges us from reality. Our mundane experience in fact demonstrates that the symbol systems that influence our conduct can "connect" us to the world in productive (and perhaps even "responsible") ways. However, acknowledging the instrumental value of our symbols does not alter the fact that things and words for things *are* different, although the difference may be difficult to elucidate, as Burke recognizes:

> In being a link between us and the nonverbal, words are by the same token a screen separating us from the nonverbal—though the statement gets tangled in its own traces, since so much of the "we" that is separated from the nonverbal by the verbal would not even exist if it were not for the verbal (or for our symbolicity in general, since the same applies to the symbol systems of dance, music, painting, and the like). (5)

If language presents such difficulties, what is to be gained by dwelling on the vicissitudes of symbolic action, especially since symbols can help us negotiate the world? Lawrence Buell points out that the literary critic's habit of stressing the divergence of *verba* and *res* is not without consequence in terms of our attitude and behavior toward the environment. He notes that "to posit a disjunction between text and world is both an indispensable starting point for mature literary understanding and a move that tends to efface the world" (5). He goes on to ask, "Must literature always lead us away from the physical world, never back to it?" (11).

Clearly Buell believes that literature can, and should, lead us back to the physical world. Equally clear is that he regards the critique of what he calls "outer mimesis" as misguided and counterproductive:

> Whatever the conscious politics of the reader who espouses a philosophical antireferentialism in the domain of literary theory, that stance underrepresents the claims of the environment on humanity by banishing it from the realms of discourse except as something absent. It forbids discourse the project of evoking the natural world through verbal surrogates and thereby attempting to bond the reader to the world as well as to discourse. (102)

What allows the "verbal surrogate" or the "stylized image" (97) to "bond the reader to the world" is its capacity to evoke the natural world in a more than superficial or sheerly solipsistic manner. Thus Buell would counter the move toward linguistic skepticism with the environmental writer's ability to produce "thick description" that achieves a certain "representational density" (90, 199). Such an emphasis amounts to choosing what Buell calls a "hermeneutics of empathy" (identified with "pre-1970 new critical and myth-symbol American scholarship") over a "hermeneutics of skepticism" ("which appraises texts more in terms of what they exclude or suppress") (35).

Buell is not advocating here what is often termed "naive verbal realism." He is fully aware that our sense of the world is chiefly a construct, a fact that admittedly places an "asymptotic limit" on our environmental responsiveness (77). He concedes, "The constraints of human perception, and of art, make zero-degree interference impossible" (81). Even so, Buell argues that, all things considered, "we would be obtuse in lumping all environmental representations together as fabricated impositions" (77). Some environmental representations *are* "better" (more responsive, more responsible) than others, a point that should not be ignored or dismissed in the name of "epistemological correctness."

Our symbolic acts *can* serve to establish a sense of connection with the environment. A pragmatic environmental poetics such as described in the previous chapter works to produce the symbols by which a new and more responsible environmental ethic is to be constituted. At the same time, such a poetics acknowledges, either implicitly or explicitly, the limitations that human perception and language place on mimetic ambitions. By creating discursive space for alternative perspectives, a pragmatic environmental poetics can also counter the "entelechial principle." As Burke notes, our "terministic compulsion" is checked, to a certain extent, when our "schemes get in one another's way" (*Language* 19). Such "interference" serves an "epistemological" goal in that it reigns in the authority of any particular symbolic regime; it also serves an ecocentric ethic by acknowledging that our perception of the (human and) nonhuman world is conditioned by language and culture.

Unmediated Perception and Environmental Poetics

When a sedate content the spirit feels,
And no fierce light disturbs, whilst it reveals,
But silent musings urge the mind to seek,
Something too high for syllables to speak . . .

—ANNE FINCH, "A Nocturnal Reverie"

Let us destroy all such artificial barriers we put up between
Nature and ourselves, for it is only when they are removed
that we see into the living heart of Nature and live with it—
which is the real meaning of love. For this, therefore, the clearing away of
all conceptual scaffolds is imperative.

—DAISETZ T. SUZUKI, "Love of Nature"

A pragmatic environmental poetics arises out of a belief that the "responsible" (and in Frost's parlance, *discreet*) deployment of symbols serves to establish a more responsive, and epistemologically adequate, attitude toward environmental discourse. If the goal of an environmental poetics is to create in human beings a sense of connection and receptivity to their environment, the discreet use of appropriately qualified symbolic regimes generated by a pragmatic poetics can do the job, as Lawrence Buell and others are right to insist.

If, however, we entertain seriously the notion that human beings are capable of perceiving the world independent of the mediating influence of linguistic structure, and in a way that produces a sense of profound intimacy with their environment, the adequacy of even a pragmatic environmental poetics may be questioned. For if such a mode of perception were possible, and if it did result in connecting us more fully and more responsively to our surroundings, it would accomplish the goal of environmental poetics without the necessary "distortion" of perception mediated by "terministic screens." Such a poetics would have the virtue of being grounded in a more "realistic" experience of the world.

What, then, are the prospects for unmediated perception? It is, in the first place, a proposition that is challenged by Burke's linguistic analysis, his concern over the claim of language on our thinking and our actions. Burke's concern is echoed, of course, by those who would sentence us to hard time in the "prison-house of language" with no possibility for parole.[2] And for his part, Robert Frost also seems to regard human perception as inescapably composed of and by linguistic structures, and specifically the structure of the metaphor. Writing in 1931, Frost confessed, "I have wanted in late years to go further and further in making metaphor the whole of thinking."[3]

But is metaphor "the whole of thinking"? In his book *Mind of Winter*, William Bevis makes the case for unmediated perception and argues, moreover, that at least one American poet, Wallace Stevens, "experimented with, or at least marvelously imitated, a meditative state of consciousness" that eluded the claims of language (5). If there is resistance to the idea of unmediated perception, observes Bevis, such resistance largely reflects, first, a "cultural bias against passivity" and, second, the prejudice of a society that has almost no tradition of meditative consciousness (39).

From the perspective of such a culture, the idea of unmediated perception looks, at best, like a contradiction in terms and, most probably, like an exotic sham. But Bevis points out that, to the contrary, "A *meditative state of consciousness* is a naturally occurring physiological phenomenon, possible for any person in any culture and probably experienced by everyone to some degree" (11–12; original emphasis). It is only trained incapacity that allows such a state of consciousness to be categorically dismissed.[4]

The crux of Bevis's argument lies in his distinction between metaphoric and meditative perception. Metaphoric perception is rooted in a Romantic sensibility and produces "a world actively, imaginatively perceived":

> In the act of creative perception, the active, imaginative self cooperates with the other to create a third category, a higher reality, the interface of self and other. A direct descendant of Kant and Coleridge, cross-bred with impressionist art and reborn in Nietzsche, this reality is the world-as-perceived, made half of objects and half of our need and use of them, a world half objective. (9)

Where metaphoric perception makes a virtue out of the active imagination, meditative perception relies on a more "passive" engagement with the world. Such passivity is traditionally seen as corresponding to a diminishment of the self or ego. "Meditative perception . . . encounters a new world by means of less self, while imaginative perception creates a new world by means of more self" (11).

In terms of the self, then, the difference between Romantic poetry and a poetry grounded in meditative perception is quite stark. We need only consider Wordsworth on the nature of poetry and the role of the poet to throw this difference into relief. To think of poetry as "the spontaneous overflow of powerful feelings" is obviously to underscore the role of the feeling self in the creative process. And even though such powerful feelings are "recollected in tranquillity," they are to be contemplated until "by a species of reaction the tranquillity gradually disappears, and an emotion, kindred to that which was before the subject of contemplation, is gradually produced, and does itself actually exist in the mind" (423). Tranquillity is thus not an end in itself but a means of recovering powerful feeling, an excited self.

Furthermore, Wordsworth argues that the poet is distinguished by his (or her) uncommon capacity for energetic feeling:

> He is a man speaking to men: a man, it is true, endued with more lively sensibility, more enthusiasm and tenderness, who has a greater knowledge of human nature, and a more comprehensive soul, than are supposed to be common among mankind; a man pleased with his own passions and volitions, and who rejoices more than other men in the spirit of life that is in him; delighting to contemplate similar volitions and passions as manifested in the goings-on of the universe, and habitually impelled to create them where he does not find them. (418–419)

The Romantic sensibility is thus heavily invested in an excited self, one charged with discovering excitement even if it must create it where it does not naturally reside.

The distinction between metaphoric and meditative consciousness, between a poetry of more self and a poetry of less self, might be interesting on its own terms but only tangentially related to a discussion of environmental poetics were it not for the fact that meditative states of consciousness are associated with experiences of intense intimacy with the phenomenal world and thus the environment. From a strictly linguistic point of view, this is, in a sense, a logical inevitability. As Bevis notes:

> It is the self that is increasingly passive in meditative experience, and when one's self is lost, how can there be a sense of anything other than self? The two concepts, self and other, are mutually dependent. To lose self is to lose other, and if there is no self and no other, then all may seem one. (50)

The experience of meditative consciousness goes beyond the realignment of syntactical categories, however. The powerful claim of the meditative experience is that it disconnects us from the abstractions of language and, in the process, reveals "a world that shrinks to an immediate whole" (145). Although such experiences are often regarded as "transcendent," the experience of meditative consciousness is in reality the opposite of transcendence; language may be surmounted or disengaged, but not nature or the mundane. Bevis argues that

> self-loss need not imply a transcendence of time and space; it may designate a sense of being, here and now, in a vivid time and space, without the thoughts and desires that define the self. Sensory meditation experience, instead of stressing nothing, stresses suchness, the thing itself perceived in a special poverty, accompanied by a special detachment that is not ennui. (68)

If it is the goal of environmental literature to put us back "in touch" with our phenomenal world, a literature that could somehow exploit the experience of meditative consciousness would seem to demand careful consideration. In short, the "stylized image" may not be the only path back to nature.

If the experience of meditative consciousness is indeed universally available, and if it produces such a sense of extraordinary intimacy with the world, we may well ask why it is not more common.

One answer has already been suggested: many cultures may not be inclined to recognize or facilitate the experience. A second, perhaps related, answer also may deserve credence. It may be the case that, in a culture fixated on exciting the self, people may come to regard the experience of less self as abnormal and perhaps threatening. If this is true, our enthusiasm for symbolic action, what Stevens called our "motive for metaphor," may indeed represent a type of compulsive avoidance behavior. According to Bevis, Stevens apparently felt that underlying this motive is ultimately "a desire to escape from a final reality 'immenser than/A poet's metaphors,' [and] a desire to shrink from 'The weight of primary noon/The ABC of being'" (149).[5] Whether we regard the experience of "suchness" or "final reality" as desirable or threatening is, or course, crucial to the prospects for a poetics grounded in the dissolution of metaphoric consciousness.[6]

In either case, the potential for experience unmediated by language does not immediately suggest the structure of a poetics with which it might be implicated. Bevis argues that meditative consciousness "is typically expressed through pure image" whereas "imaginative perception" finds its expression through metaphor (11). Or again: "Metaphor, especially dazzling metaphor, is the quintessential language of the mind. The clear image or pure ultimate abstraction ('chairs,' 'nothing,' 'all,' 'whole') is the quintessential language of no-mind" (146). Such talk is not altogether unfamiliar to modern poetic theory; it brings to mind, to a certain extent, the rhetoric of Imagism and its emphasis on "direct treatment," "economy of words," and the like. Of course, Imagism also *contrasted* the "clear image" and "pure ultimate abstraction" ostensibly in favor of the latter. (Pound: "Go in fear of abstractions.") While an austere rhetoric may be associated with experiences of meditative consciousness, it is not clear that it or *any* rhetoric can escape the entanglements of language. As Burke has suggested, *every* terminology invokes discriminations. Thus Bevis may be faithfully describing artistic *conventions* when he asserts:

> For artists, the suchness of meditative perception has most usually encouraged an emphasis on the single image (not a symbol or metaphor), or the single perception, exploding fantasy or thought. The clear image is regarded sometimes with exclamation, but always with a noninterpretive detachment. (62)

In terms of the operations of language, however, the distinctions he makes among image, perception, symbol, and metaphor are without much difference. It may be somewhat reductionist to categorize all such linguistic structures as *terms*, but inasmuch as they are constructed out of words, they are not immune to the vicissitudes incurred by all terminologies. On this analysis, a rhetoric of meditative experience thus remains a conventional fiction, useful perhaps, but essentially divorced from the experience it "represents."[7]

In an important sense, then, the horizon of unmediated perception also marks the horizon of poetry. To engage the resources of poetry is to engage in symbolic action and therefore to abandon the experience of egolessness and nondiscrimination. Must we then, in order to keep faith with the experience of meditative consciousness, banish poetry from the kingdom? While Plato argued that artistic representation suffers for being twice removed from transcendental reality, is not the fact that the poem is even *once* removed from phenomenal experience reason enough to send all "nature poets" packing?[8]

What seems to be called for is not so much rhetorical *austerity* as rhetorical *abstinence*. Although the notion may at first seem a bit odd, instances of rhetorical abstention are in fact not that difficult to discover. It is a relatively common practice, for example, to offer a "moment of silence" in memory of the deceased and as a gesture of respect. One might argue that, in terms of environmental poetry, such self-restraint would demonstrate the profoundest respect for the ontological autonomy of the existential universe. Such restraint would thus serve an ecocentric ethic by acknowledging that the nonhuman world exists independently of human desire, including the desire for representation.

Rhetorical abstinence is also an important aspect of Islamic aesthetics. I refer, of course, to the well-known prohibition of images that, in the strictest sense, applies only to the image of God. As Titus Burckhardt points out, this prohibition derives from the Decalogue and is in opposition to idolatrous polytheism. Images of God are to be avoided on the theory that "any plastic representation of the divinity is . . . the distinctive mark of the error which associates the relative with the Absolute, or the created with the Uncreated, by reducing the one to the level of the other" (27). According to some sects, however, the prohibition of images (formally speaking, *aniconism*) extends to any entity capable of casting a shadow. Thus, "In Sunni Arab circles, the representation of any living being is frowned upon, because of respect for the divine secret contained within every creature" (29).

Islamic aniconism is not a perfect example of rhetorical abstinence, however, to the extent that while representation is eschewed in the simplest mimetic sense, some forms *are* presented, typically the complex geometric designs for which Islamic art and architecture are renowned. One might suppose that even on this level such forms partake of a "grammar" or a "rhetoric" by virtue of which they are differentiated and "articulated." Even so, Burckhardt argues that the geometric pattern in Islamic art

> may be no more than the quite silent exteriorization, as it were, of a contemplative state, and in this case—or in this respect—it reflects no ideas, but transforms the surroundings qualitatively, by having them share in an equilibrium whose centre of gravity is the unseen.

> In this respect, the function of Islamic art is analogous to that of virgin nature, especially the desert, which is likewise favourable to contemplation, although in another respect the order created by art opposes the chaos of desert landscape.
>
> The proliferation of decoration in Muslim art does not contradict this quality of contemplative emptiness; on the contrary, ornamentation with abstract forms enhances it through its unbroken rhythm and its endless interweaving. Instead of ensnaring the mind and leading it into some imaginary world, it dissolves mental "fixations," just as contemplation of a running stream, a flame, or leaves quivering in the wind, can detach consciousness from its inward "idols." (27–29)

Burckhardt correctly acknowledges that even abstract or nonrepresentational art, by virtue of the fact that it is the product of aesthetic discriminations, necessarily distinguishes itself from the "chaos" of the natural world. Consequently, to the degree that aniconism is "formal" it turns from rhetorical abstinence toward rhetorical austerity.

It is useful, in this context, to distinguish aniconism from its more pugnacious counterpart, *iconoclasm*. Where aniconism shies away from mimesis toward (something like) representational austerity or asceticism, iconoclasm pursues the *destruction* of the image. In this regard, Buell's critique of the "hermeneutics of skepticism" is an attack on the iconoclastic bent of some contemporary (eco)critical theory, habits of thought that serve only to deconstruct in order to dismantle our "stylized images" of the natural world. On Buell's account, such iconoclasm merely succeeds in further estranging us from our environment.

I would like to argue, to the contrary, that an environmental poetics informed by linguistic skepticism can serve to establish a more intimate and responsive relationship toward nature. By emphasizing the essential distinction between things and our words for things, a skeptical hermeneutic acknowledges the ontological autonomy of the nonhuman. A skeptical hermeneutic thus encourages, to whatever extent possible, an *awareness* of nonhuman entities unmediated by linguistic structure. I would also argue that an environmental poetics informed by a skeptical hermeneutics reinforces ecocentric values by recognizing that nonhuman entities do not exist merely in their relation to human interpretive structures or as material for poetic representation.

Référance *and Skeptical Environmental Poetics*

O swallows, swallows, poems are not
The point. Finding again the world,
That is the point, where loveliness
Adorns intelligible things
Because the mind's eye lit the sun.

—HOWARD NEMEROV, "The Blue Swallows"

In his recent, groundbreaking study, *Sustainable Poetry*, Leonard Scigaj argues a similar thesis and offers a nuanced and thorough elucidation of what I am referring to here as a skeptical environmental poetics. Scigaj asks the rhetorical question, "Can nature ever be anything more than an impossibly alien 'other,' trapped in a dualistic paradigm, that humans must subjectivize and personify, imbue with human qualities, in order to understand?" Scigaj believes, correctly, that one aspect of the nature-writing tradition offers a responsible alternative:

> Nature and environmental poets often record moments of nondualistic inhabitation in specific places where the experience occurs only when the noise of human ratiocination, including the fabrications of language, has been silenced or revel in moments of phenomenological participation in Being where the activity of seeing intertwines the human and nonhuman worlds. (8)

Crucially, this intertwining of the human and nonhuman attenuates the claims of language on our environmental experience. The poets Scigaj admires affirm that "human language is much more limited than the ecological processes of nature and [use] postmodern self-reflexivity to disrupt the fashionably hermetic treatment of poetry as a self-contained linguistic construct whose ontological ground is language theory" (11).

Scigaj argues that "ecopoetry" and "environmental poetry" are largely products of the `ast thirty years and represent a rejection of, and alternative to, poststructural language theory.

Like Buell, Scigaj is responding to a "postmodern" critical environment that seems to take as a matter of faith the hegemony of language and the impossibility of the referential object (namely, the more-than-human world). According to Scigaj, those he identifies as "ecopoets"

> are not indifferent to language or to poststructural critiques of the function of language. They argue the reverse of the poststructural position that all experience is mediated by language. For ecopoets language is an instrument that the poet continually refurbishes to articulate his originary experience in nature. . . . For the ecopoet, language preserves the historical record of the percept. (29–30)

Although their strategies for articulating unmediated environmental experience are ultimately different, Scigaj finds in the poetry of Ammons, Berry, Merwin, and Snyder a common poetics, which, while acknowledging "the fabrications of language," seeks to keep faith with originary perception and experience.[9]

Scigaj captures the spirit and essential strategies of a skeptical environmental poetics in the term *référance:*

> I believe that the adequate term for this process that has often occurred in the last thirty years of ecopoetry is *référance,* from the French verb *se référer,* which means "to relate or refer oneself to." In

> practice, *référance* turns the reader's gaze toward an apprehension of the cyclic processes of wild nature after a self-reflexive recognition of the limits (the *sous nature*) of language. After this two-stage process, a third moment often occurs, the moment of atonement with nature, where we confide our trust in (*s'en référer*) nature's rhythms and cycles, where reading nature becomes our text. In other words, a text informed by *référance*, by the interdisciplinary practices of ecological and environmental poetry, involves (1) reaching a self-reflexive acknowledgment of the limits of language, (2) referring one's perceptions beyond the printed page to nature, to the referential origin of all language, and (3) in most cases achieving an atonement or at-one-ment with nature. (38)[10]

The processes circumscribed by *référance* allow for both the nondualistic experience of environmental interconnectedness and reciprocity and its expression within the comprehensive confines of language. For Scigaj, *référance* articulates not merely a practice that is faithful to the ecopoet's epistemological and aesthetic commitments and his or her unmediated experience of a living world but also to the respect and awe such experience engenders. Such "epiphanic" experience is by nature necessarily ecocentric and by design linguistically humbling.

A poem that begins to illustrate some of the possibilities of *référence* and a skeptical environmental poetics is Adrienne Rich's "Rural Reflections":

> This is the grass your feet are planted on.
> You paint it orange or you sing it green,
>   But you have never found
> A way to make the grass mean what you mean.
>
> A cloud can be whatever you intend:
> Ostrich or leaning tower or staring eye.
>   But you have never found
> A cloud sufficient to express the sky.

Get out there with your splendid expertise;
Raymond who cuts the meadow does no less.
        Inhuman nature says:
Inhuman patience is the true success.

Human impatience trips you as you run;
        Stand still and you must lie.
It is the grass that cuts the mower down;
It is the cloud that swallows up the sky.

        (*Snapshots* 13)

The first stanza of this poem insists on the divergence of meaning (as the product of our interpretive and representational acts, here painting and singing) and the "thing" that is the object of meaning (the referent of the noun "grass"). All we can do, the poem suggests, is to present *attributes* of the thing (nouns themselves, adjectives, "orange," "green"), which are not, finally, the thing itself: "But you have never found/A way to make the grass mean what you mean." The object of representation remains stubbornly recalcitrant to representational effort. Moreover, on a deeper level the object remains nonidentical to representation even when the given attribute corresponds to our conventional expectations, as when we sing the grass green. The poem explicitly lumps such conventional description in with unconventional description ("paint it orange"); both remain equally divorced from their referent.

"A cloud can be whatever you intend:/Ostrich or leaning tower or staring eye." These lines point to the power of the imagination to shape the perception of phenomena in the direction of our will or desire. But here, imaginative power, while fertile, is ultimately unable to represent the totality of experience. It can manage *figures* (clouds) but is at a loss when it comes to representing the *ground* of figuration (the sky).

The poem then urges (taunts?) us into the scene, the field of representation, with our "splendid expertise" (most literally, painting and singing, by extension the poet's proficiency at representation). Such proficiency is equivalent to that of "Raymond who cuts the meadow," perhaps because both activities (mowing, representing) amount to gross manipulation (and probably *reduction*, in that the grass is "reduced," cut down, just as the object is "reduced," rendered into its attributes). In contrast to these manipulative activities, the poem presents a nonhuman ontology that puts a premium on passivity: "Inhuman nature says:/Inhuman patience is the true success."

On the other hand, "Human impatience trips you as you run." If "human impatience" can be read as referring to our seeming compulsion for representation, then the activity of representation trips us up as the movement of meaning, from signified to signifier, necessarily takes us down.

But what is this "inhuman patience," then? It would seem to imply, first of all, the denial of our unique nature as "symbol-using animals." But inasmuch as Rich is here pointing to something that may in fact be available to the human species, I believe her to mean by "inhuman patience" a kind of representational restraint informed by linguistic skepticism. Such restraint would serve to acknowledge the limitations of symbolic action. But representational restraint informed by linguistic skepticism serves more than an epistemological goal. Representational restraint can also be an ethical act, one that stresses the distinction between word and thing in the name of focusing our attention on the thing itself, free of symbolic mediation and "manipulation."

In the movement from unmediated perception to the medium of language, however, the poet confronts the dilemma of symbolic action. The iconoclast exists, in a sense, to subvert this movement. "Rural Reflections" is iconoclastic to the extent that it moves to restrain the attempt to make nature "mean what [we] mean." What it offers in place of our representations is nature on its own terms, that is, free of terministic screens.[11]

A poem such as "Rural Reflections" is successful only to the extent that it creates the possibility of meditative perception. Such perception is necessarily divorced from either the writing or the reading of the poem. At best, Rich may encourage us to put down her book and go out-of-doors into a real field. As Scigaj puts it, in *référance* the poet underlines the primary function of ecopoetry "to point us *outward*, toward that infinitely less limited referential reality of nature" (38). The true complement to an environmental poetics that embraces linguistic skepticism is its implementation outside of poetry.

Référance integrates linguistic skepticism into an environmental poetics to produce a poetry nuanced in its treatment of both metaphorical and meditative consciousness. *Référance* also better represents the real motion of the mind. As Bevis reminds us, the state of meditative perception is unstable, and our response to the world cannot be confined to unmediated experience:

> Any supposed opposition between ordinary and meditative states of consciousness, however, must be placed in perspective: all states of consciousness are temporary. We cannot be awake all the time, dream all the time, or meditate all the time. Biologically, states of consciousness are complementary, not exclusive. (158)

The mind's fluctuations suggest a poetry that stages the interplay of metaphorical and meditative consciousness. It moves beyond mere solipsism, however, to the extent that its meditative component admits an autonomous world free of mediating influences. Thus, it is a poetry that looks in two directions at once: toward the signs for things, and toward the things upon which we hang our signs.

To conclude this discussion, I would like to turn to "Reading Lao Tzu Again in the New Year," a poem by Charles Wright that

I believe puts into practice the skeptical environmental poetics described above:

> Snub end of a dismal year,
> deep in the dwarf orchard,
> The sky with its undercoat of blackwash and point stars,
> I stand in the dark and answer to
> My life, this shirt I want to take off,
> which is on fire . . .
>
> Old year, new year, old song, new song,
> nothing will change hands
> Each time we change heart, each time
> Like a hard cloud that has drifted all day through the sky
> Toward the night's shrugged shoulder
> with its epaulet of stars.
>
> ———
>
> Prosodies rise and fall.
> Structures rise in the mind and fall.
> Failure reseeds the old ground.
> Does the grass, with its inches in two worlds, love the dirt?
> Does the snowflake the raindrop?
>
> I've heard that those who know will never tell us,
> and heard
> That those who tell us will never know.
> Words are wrong.
> Structures are wrong.
> Even the questions are compromise.
>
> Desire discriminates and language discriminates:
> They form no part of the essence of all things:
> each word
> Is a failure, each object
> We name and place
> leads us another step away from the light.

Loss is its own gain.
                              Its secret is emptiness.
Our images lie in the flat pools of their dark selves
Like bodies of water the tide moves.
They move as the tide moves.
                                        Its secret is emptiness.

Four days into January,
                              the grass grows tiny, tiny
Under the peach trees.
Wind from the Blue Ridge tumbles the hat
Of daylight farther and farther
                                        into the eastern counties.

Sunlight spray on the ash limbs.
                                        Two birds
Whistle at something unseen, one black note and one interval.
We're placed between now and not-now,
                                                  held by affection,
Large rock balanced upon a small rock.

(4)

The beginning of this poem establishes a narrative line, the poet standing in a "dwarf orchard" under the stars: "I stand in the dark and answer to/My life, this shirt I want to take off,/which is on fire." What follows is, in a sense, his answer. His first response is to observe the circle of life and of poetry ("Old year, new year, old song, new song"), intimating a frustration with the recapitulation of both time and language ("nothing will change hands"). The figure Wright chooses to express this complicated feeling ("each time/Like a hard cloud") is as ambiguous as it is extravagant. The poet seems caught up in the beautiful language of poetry as he struggles for an "answer" to his life.

As if conscious of its own rhetorical excess, the poem shifts radically in both focus and tone. Short, declarative sentences focus now on language, on the poet's struggle for meaning in the forms of poetry: "Prosodies rise and fall./Structures rise in the mind and fall./Failure reseeds the old ground." Given the inconstancy of language, Wright then wonders what can we really know of the world. "Does the grass, with its inches in two worlds, love the dirt?/Does the snowflake the raindrop?" He then states the dilemma of language, paraphrasing Lao-tzu: "I've heard that those who know will never tell us,/and heard/That those who tell us will never know."

What follows is a manifesto on linguistic skepticism:

> Words are wrong.
> Structures are wrong.
> Even the questions are compromise.
>
> Desire discriminates and language discriminates:
> They form no part of the essence of all things:
> each word
>
> Is a failure, each object
> We name and place
> leads us another step away from the light.

At this point the poet might as well give up and go back inside. But the poem does not end here. Wright seems to have discovered at least one answer to the question of his life. Significantly, his "answer" takes the form of an insight into the limitations of knowledge and especially of representation:

> Loss is its own gain.
> Its secret is emptiness.
> Our images lie in the flat pools of their dark selves
> Like bodies of water the tide moves.
> They move as the tide moves.
> Its secret is emptiness.

Desire creates the need for significance and signification. But "Our images lie," and only our recognition of that reveals the essential emptiness of our words.

Having exceeded the dilemma of language, the poem now moves beyond even this void, back to the world of phenomena and poetry. The final section begins by reentering the scene, some days having passed. The focus is tight, the voice muted: "the grass grows tiny, tiny/Under the peach trees." But then Wright risks a figure that resonates all the more coming as it does "out of the void": "Wind from the Blue Ridge tumbles the hat/of daylight farther and farther/into the eastern counties." Modulating once again, the poem turns "imagistic," economical, the emphasis on visual detail. The line "Sunlight spray on the ash limbs" recalls Pound's "In a Station of the Metro." It serves as a bridge from the figure of the hat to the poem's final turns, three "forms" of the poet's final "answer":

> Two birds
> Whistle at something unseen, one black note and one interval.
> We're placed between now and not-now,
> held by affection,
> Large rock balanced upon a small rock.

The contrast between the poem's figures and its nod toward the void energizes both and encourages a reading that attends to both what can be said and what cannot. What materializes from the fields of phenomena and language is consequently thrown into high relief. The final image ("Large rock balanced upon a small rock"), potentially quite ordinary, instead resonates with all the energy of the poem, standing in good stead for the answer to the poet's life.

I believe that Wright, and poets who engage a similar poetics, crafts an approach to the environment that is responsible enough to be informed by the recalcitrance the nonhuman realm offers to our representations of it, an approach that keeps faith with our need to know our world within the limits of symbolic representation, as well as with the objects of such knowing, without subjecting them to the forged charm of metaphor.

I began this chapter by proposing to look at Robert Frost's "Two Look at Two" as paradigmatic of our encounter with the nonhuman. Across the "tangled wall" of human invention, our worlds meet, reflected in the vision we bring to bear. Our words reach across that wall and become lost in the void that separates language from reality. With some effort, by standing still, listening, we can call them back.

> And beyond the days, beyond the slow-foot letters
> of the nights, the actual, universal strength,
> without a word of rhetoric—there it is.
>
> —WALLACE STEVENS,
> "Repetitions of a Young Captain"

AFTERWORD

Politics and Environmental Poetics

When I began this study, my office was on the second floor of the tallest building on the University of Oregon campus, a structure that also houses the departments of English, history, sociology, philosophy, economics, and comparative literature, as well as the Humanities Center. If I climbed to the seventh floor and looked through the windows of a seminar room that was usually unlocked, I was often rewarded with a fine view of the university with its manicured lawns and stately trees. Farther east, the Cascade range rose, its snow-capped summits visible when weather permitted (and when the grass seed farmers refrained from burning the stubble in their vast fields to the north).

Below those peaks lies the most "productive" forest in the United States. Wave after wave of logging has stripped entire slopes of their trees, leaving vast swaths of blasted ground and snarled slash baking in the summer heat. In the towns that dot the flank of the Cascades, trees are processed into lumber and veneer and paper, products very much in evidence in the typical academic office, including my own. As the remaining ancient trees are consumed, the mills close one by one; the industry is shifting south to stands of tropical timber and back to the maturing monoculture forests of the southeastern states.

One morning, as I was readying an early draft of this book, the radio announced the ravaging by fire of hundreds of thousands of acres of forest in the central and eastern parts of the state. To the south, in California, the lights flickered and went out—the second large-scale power failure of the summer. The unusually hot weather caused high-voltage lines to sag; when they touched the trees below they arced, jolting the grid from Mexico to Canada. Crews kept themselves busy cutting down hundreds of trees that posed a threat to the system. To the north, on the great dams of the Columbia, the Bonneville Power Administration dedicated more water to electrical generation to satisfy an increased demand for power. Water was diverted from spillways and fish ladders. Some scientists and environmentalists predicted that 18,000 endangered chinook could perish each day they were forced to negotiate the steel turbine blades of the electrical generators or were compelled to circle endlessly at the base of dry ladders. An industry spokesman estimated that less than ten fish were likely to die during the period of increased energy production.

Ravaged forests. Dying salmon. In *Imagining the Earth*, John Elder argues that "poetry's task is to ground human culture once more on a planet rich in nonhuman life and beauty" (26). It is a noble sentiment, made nobler as the world around us becomes less rich and less beautiful with the destruction of forests, rivers, and other ecosystems. But what can poetry really hope to accomplish in the face of environmental devastation and extraordinary rates of extinction? How can an art that is considerably marginalized in the public sphere alter the bearings of a culture bent on destruction? Do we have reason, at this late date, to believe, with Eliot, that poetry "makes a difference to the speech, to the sensibility, to the lives of all the members of a society, to all the members of the community, to the whole people, whether they read and enjoy poetry or not: even, in fact, whether they know the names of their greatest poets or not" ("Social" 12; Elder 210)?

To the extent that humanity is presently reevaluating its relationship to the nonhuman world, poets are contributing to the effort by offering both novel and time-honored metaphors as alternatives to the concepts and attitudes that accompany environmental destruction. Even so, to many people Nature remains merely a resource to be exploited, raw material for human ambitions. But to others, Nature is mother, lover, friend, the real polis, the web of being and becoming. If our hope is to minimize environmental destruction while working to establish something like "balance" with the nonhuman, the prospect for success arguably rests with the production of more responsible metaphors to live by, and their extensive propagation.

While I have supreme faith in the ability of poets to generate the figures that might shape a better world, I am far less sanguine concerning poetry's ostensible power to move through the world with strength and grace enough to change minds and hearts. Other rhetorical acts, especially those that command a larger audience than does poetry, are likely to be more effective in transforming the way we approach the nonhuman. Strategically speaking, television, film, and the popular press, while relying on what might be called the "poetic impulse" for their content, are in a better position to reach enough people to make enough of a difference.

Strictly in terms of its propagandistic utility, the problem with poetry—and its greatest virtue—is that it depends for its vitality both on the invention of live figures and, even more, on a genuinely precocious attitude toward the language that forms them. By "precocious" I mean the qualities expressed in the constellation of its synonyms: advanced, apt, bright, gifted, intelligent. To a species trained by and large to exercise only the most rudimentary and utilitarian aspects of language, the precocious deployment of metaphor (literature in general and, at its most precocious, poetry) seems unnecessarily burdensome as it smacks of obfuscation and elitism.

If the solution to environmental crisis requires, in Lawrence Buell's words again, "finding better ways of imaging nature and humanity's relation to it," and such imaging involved the "poetic impulse" only in terms of striking the right metaphors, I would be content to urge it on wherever and whenever it managed to confront the senseless degradation of our natural world. My suspicion is, however, that Buell is only partially right. I think we need to go further and recognize that the "crisis of the imagination" that underlies environmental crisis has less to do with the particularities of our imaginations than it does with the vicissitudes of imaginative acts themselves. To put the matter bluntly: inventing "better ways of imaging nature and humanity's relation to it" may in fact be the easy part, an enterprise that comes naturally to poets, contemporary or otherwise; understanding both the strengths and limitations of imaginative acts, however, and creating a poetic practice that incorporates this understanding in the name of environmental redemption, is a much more difficult project.

The poetry that engages what I have called a skeptical environmental poetics recognizes the border between language and the living world as a frontier beyond which abides the truly wild. To acknowledge that such a frontier exists is not to doubt either the potential utility or the potential radiance of language; instead, it is to begin to develop an awareness that respects the immediacy and complexity of an evolving world that lies always just beyond the grasp of language.

Some will argue that such a poetics silences and erases nature once more, just as the nonhuman is finding a strong voice and a strong presence in the songs of our poets. I am sympathetic to such an objection, particularly as it concerns aspects of nature I am unlikely to encounter on my own. Who can forget Lawrence's whales burning with life "in the blue deep bed of the sea," "the maelstrom-tip" of "the whale's strong phallus," the "enormous mother whales dreaming suckling their whale-tender young / and dreaming with strange whale eyes wide open in the waters of the beginning and the end" (16–17)? We are awed by such creatures, grow tender toward them, feel we know them, worry about their future.

But should we dive with whales, should we be fortunate enough to experience these creatures in their own world, we do well to leave behind the musings of whale-poets like Lawrence, for to cling to poetry serves only to banish us from the wilderness we hope to enter. The best poets of nature understand the full extent of our exile. They know that wilderness rises up in every natural fact. And though we domesticate the world in the poetry of whales and salmon and trees, something wild remains, inextricable, precious. To lose the living things of the world, they know, is to lose the wilderness each has to offer. They know that to lose the living things of the world is to accept the self-exile of language, as if we had no choice, forgetting the way back, because nothing there abides.

NOTES

Introduction

1. Of course, the origins of anglophone "nature poetry" predate the neoclassical period; its roots can be found in Celtic, Norse, and Anglo-Saxon traditions and especially in the Greek and Latin pastoral traditions. Raymond Williams notes that "nature poetry" as we have come to know it derives from descriptions of nature in the pastoral and that our modern approach to such description is itself the product of a shift in perspective (and ethos) from the observations of "the working countryman" to that of "the scientist or tourist" (Gifford 3).

2. John Elder's recent *Reading the Mountains of Home* (Cambridge: Harvard University Press, 1998), a book-length treatment of Frost's "Directive" in the context of Elder's personal experience of the Hogback Anticlinc in Vermont's Green Mountains, suggests that Frost's stock may already be on the rise within some ecocritical circles.

Chapter 1. Toward a Rhetoric of Ecological Poetics

1. The opening lines of this chapter are drawn from Kenneth Burke's "Dialetician's Hymn," in *Language as Symbolic Action: Essays on Life, Literature, and Method* (Berkeley: University of California Press, 1966), 55–57.

2. For a very brief summary of the Sophistic tradition, see Thomas Conley, *Rhetoric in the European Tradition* (New York: Longman, 1990),

4–7. For a spirited defense of the Sophists, see Susan Jarratt, *Rereading the Sophists: Classical Rhetoric Refigured* (Carbondale: Southern Illinois University Press, 1991).

3. See, for example, Sara Dunn and Alan Scholefield, eds., *Beneath the Wide Wide Heaven: Poetry of the Environment from Antiquity to the Present* (London: Virago Press, 1991). For a somewhat older collection of ecological/environmental poetry spanning several millennia, see Robert Bly, ed., *News of the Universe: Poems of Twofold Consciousness* (San Francisco: Sierra Club Books, 1980).

4. Bly, *News of the Universe*, esp. 30–37.

5. This sketch of the principles of ecological science is drawn largely from Putman and Wratten, *Principles of Ecology* (Berkeley: University of California Press, 1984).

6. I do not want to leave the impression that all ecological scientists are engaged in fighting a rearguard action against the degradation of ecology by the unwashed masses. Witness, for example, the commotion caused by E. O. Wilson's forays into sociobiology, or the furor surrounding Lovelock's "Gaia Hypothesis," eminent scientists both.

7. An ecocentric environmental ethic is typically distinguished from egocentric, homocentric, and androcentric ethics. Egocentric ethics derive normative claims from concepts of the self and aim toward what is good for the individual. A homocentric (or humanistic) ethic regards nature as ultimately serving, in some fashion, human interests (whether socioeconomic, philosophical, psychological, or spiritual). Ecocentric ethics, in contrast, refuse to privilege humanity on any grounds and resist construing nonhuman nature as a means to human ends. For the ecocentric critique of egocentric and homocentric environmental ethics, see especially Bill Devall and George Sessions, *Deep Ecology* (Salt Lake City: Peregrine Smith, 1985).

Homocentric and, to a certain extent, ecocentric environmental ethics have been susceptible to a feminist critique that finds an androcentric bias to both. For a good overview of these terms, and the specifically ecofeminist perspective, see Carolyn Merchant, *Radical Ecology: The Search for a Livable World* (New York: Routledge, 1992), esp. 102–108. Merchant argues for what she calls "Deepest Ecology," an ecocentric ethic that is egalitarian in terms of species, race, and gender.

8. See, for example, Paul W. Taylor, *Respect for Nature: A Theory of*

Environmental Ethics (Princeton: Princeton University Press, 1986), 51. See also Merchant, *Radical Ecology*, 78–81. For Hume's analysis, see David Hume, *A Treatise of Human Nature* (Oxford: Clarendon Press, 1960), bk. 3, pt. 3, sec. 1, 469–470. For his description of the "naturalistic fallacy," see George Edward Moore, *Principia Ethica* (Cambridge: Cambridge University Press, 1903), ch. 1, sec. B, no. 9 ff. For a classic, and lively, discussion concerning Hume's challenge to ecological ethics, see J. Baird Callicott, "Hume's *Is/Ought* Dichotomy and the Relation of Ecology to Leopold's Land Ethic," *Environmental Ethics* 4 (1982): 163–174. Also, Holmes Rolston III, "Is There an Ecological Ethic?" *Ethics* 85 (1975): 93–109; Tom Regan, "On the Connection Between Environmental Science and Environmental Ethics," *Environmental Ethics* 2 (1980): 363–366.

9. De Man's assertion that "all true criticism occurs in the mode of crisis" would seem to apply as well to revolutionary rhetoric. See "Criticism and Crisis," in *Blindness and Insight: Essays in the Rhetoric of Contemporary Criticism*, 2d ed. (Minneapolis: University of Minnesota Press, 1971, 1983), 8. Revolution is merely the most extreme mode of criticism, the partial or total transformation of the status quo.

I am reminded, too, of Frost's witticism in "A Semi-Revolution":

> I advocate a semi-revolution.
> The trouble with a total revolution
> (Ask any reputable Rosicrucian)
> Is that it brings the same class up on top.
> Executives of skillful execution
> Will therefore plan to go halfway and stop.
> Yes, revolutions are the only salves,
> But they're one thing that should be done by halves.
>
> (*A Witness Tree* 73)

10. For an analysis of the ideological implications of such lapsarian rhetoric, see Williams's *Country and the City* (New York: Oxford University Press, 1973), 57–60. See also Gifford's use of Williams in *Green Voices: Understanding Contemporary Nature Poetry* (Manchester: Manchester University Press, 1995), esp. 17–18.

11. Compare Randall Roorda's attack on John P. O'Grady's "conflation" of "'ecology' with 'the science of ecology'" in *ISLE* 4 (fall 1997): 49 n. 2.

Chapter 2. Green Speech: The Trope of Speaking Nature

1. "Nature and Silence." *Environmental Ethics* 14 (1992): 339–350.

2. This and the following *Turtle Island* passages are quoted in Max Oelschlaeger's "Wilderness, Civilization, and Language," in *The Wilderness Condition: Essays on Environment and Civilization*, edited by Max Oelschlaeger (San Francisco: Sierra Club Books, 1992), 271–308.

3. We need only note how humans wishing to exterminate their brethren tend to adopt the rhetorical strategy of representing their victims as less than bona fide subjects: as subhumans, animals, objects of disgust, and so forth.

4. The relevance of Burke's linguistic theories to environmental discourse is well established. Randall Roorda notes in his 1997 article, "KB in Green: Ecology, Critical Theory, and Kenneth Burke," *ISLE* 4 (fall 1997): 39–52, that the term "ecocriticism" itself was coined by Burke scholar William H. Rueckert in his 1978 analysis of Burke's environmentalism. While Roorda's own treatment of Burke touches on several ideas I would like to put into play here and in later chapters, especially the implications of his "Definition of Man," Roorda's essay itself centers productively on Burke's "Dramatism" and his concept of "Counter-Nature."

5. Such a category would theoretically include alinguistic humans as well as nonhuman animals.

Chapter 3. Ethos and Environmental Ethics

1. Iser argues that representation as aesthetic semblance implies an essential "doubling" action that I equate with the "rhetoricity" of the literary text. Iser identifies three modes of "doubling" that create disruptions in the textual field (whether between the text and the extratextual world or between aspects of the text itself): these include acts of selection, acts of combination, and the "disclosure" of the literary text as fiction. I think we can, without too much trouble, see these disruptions as rhetorical strategies, or the effects of the particular rhetoric employed in a given text.

2. Of course, identification through symbolic action, as in poetry, is best seen as compensatory. As Burke notes, "unification is not unity, but a compensation for disunity" (*Grammar* 173).

Chapter 4. Pragmatic Environmental Poetics

1. While ecology is plainly not synonymous with contemporaneity, it is a prominent constituent of the contemporary "scene" and may serve as metonymic of an even larger portion, intersecting as it does with systems theory, process philosophy, a resurgent nature spirituality, and politics of class, race, and gender.

2. Of course, Pope's original audience would have had its own tradition of apocalypse to draw on; perhaps these readers kept an ear out for the thundering hooves of the Four Horsemen much as the contemporary reader listens for the wail of the disaster siren.

3. W. John Coletta offers a similar critique of Pope in "The Great Web of Being: Ecological and Evolutionary Aesthetics and the Ideology of Biology" (Ph.D. diss., University of Oregon, 1989), 42–49. In place of the "Great Chain of Being," Coletta argues for the virtues, from the perspective of ecological science, of a different metaphor, "The Great Web of Being," at work in the poetry of Mary Oliver and Theodore Roethke.

4. Compare Nietzsche: "There is *only* a perspective seeing, *only* a perspective 'knowing'; and the *more* affects we allow to speak about one thing, the *more* eyes, different eyes, we can use to observe one thing, the more complete will our 'concept' of this thing, our 'objectivity,' be" (*On the Genealogy of Morals* 119).

5. See also John Gage, *In the Arresting Eye: The Rhetoric of Imagism* (Baton Rouge: Louisiana State University Press, 1981).

6. *The Postmodern Condition: A Report on Knowledge*, translated by Geoff Bennington and Brian Massumi (Minneapolis: University of Minnesota Press, 1984), xxiv.

7. Bevis argues that in terms of their poetics, the Language Poets have a lot more in common with Stevens than with Pound (*Mind of Winter* 303). Rotella's reading of Frost, Moore, and Bishop suggests that they, too, belong in the same camp with Stevens. I would like to avoid, however, viewing twentieth-century American poetry as a contest between the Pound Line and the Stevens Line. (For one thing, I think Stevens is anticipated by Frost, five years his elder, and the Frost Line has a nice, icy ring to it.) I hope to show how hermeneutical poetics, rather than representing a novel, twentieth-century development, is in fact a manifestation of certain fundamental poetic principles.

8. See *Phaedrus* 262A ff.

9. See Wayne Booth, *Modern Dogma and the Rhetoric of Assent* (Chicago: University of Chicago Press, 1974).

10. See M. M. Bakhtin, *The Dialogic Imagination*, edited by Michael Holquist, translated by Caryl Emerson and Michael Holquist (Austin: University of Texas Press, 1981).

Chapter 5. Skeptical Environmental Poetics

1. See Burke's "(Nonsymbolic) Motion/(Symbolic) Action," *Critical Inquiry* 4 (summer 1978): 809–838. The relationship between motive and symbolic action circumscribes Burke's entire oeuvre but is specifically developed in *A Grammar of Motives* and *A Rhetoric of Motives.*

2. See Frederic Jameson, *The Prison-House of Language: A Critical Account of Structuralism and Russian Formalism* (Princeton: Princeton University Press, 1972).

3. "I find some one now and then to agree with me that all thinking, except mathematical thinking, is metaphorical, or all thinking except scientific thinking. The mathematical might be difficult for me to bring in, but the scientific is easy enough" (R. Frost, "Education," 332).

4. The notion of unmediated experience has gained, or regained, some adherents even among contemporary philosophers, long trained, at least since Nietzsche and Wittgenstein, to regard experience and knowledge as necessarily mediated by language. See, for example, Edward Pols, *Radical Realism: Direct Knowing in Science and Philosophy* (Ithaca: Cornell University Press, 1992).

5. Wallace Stevens, "The Motive for Metaphor," in *The Collected Poems of Wallace Stevens* (New York: Knopf, 1978), 288.

6. In her own more recent appraisal of Stevens as a "nature poet," *Notations of the Wild: Ecology in the Poetry of Wallace Stevens* (Iowa City: University of Iowa Press, 1997), Gyorgyi Voros argues that while Stevens "sought to write a new Nature poetry that answered to what he perceived to be a great lack in American consciousness—a sense of the immediacy and profound presence of earth itself, rock-bottom foundation of human thought and experience," the expression of such a sense of immediacy and presence is necessarily refracted though the contingencies of language (6).

In a statement reminiscent of Burke's treatment of "terministic screens," Voros points to a passage in "Notes toward a Supreme Fiction," noting that "Stevens acknowledges the impossibility, for a human being, of seeing anything in its 'essential barrenness,' since all human experience is necessarily filtered through a set of perceptions circumscribed by biology and, more important, usually expressed in language which is paradoxically both route to, and barrier between the individual and whatever is objectively 'real'" (54).

7. "And since the mystic communicates ultimately in terms of the oxymoron (the figure that combines contradictory elements within a single expression), we should see in the packing of an image or idea with divergent motives a more or less remote instance of 'literary mysticism.' "In a sense, of course, literary mysticism is a contradiction in terms. For as James points out, the mystic's experience is 'ineffable.' But poetry being expressive, mystic poetry would thus have to 'express the ineffable'—and to do that it would have to be what Kant might have called a *Seindes Unding*." (Burke, *Rhetoric*, 324)

8. *Republic* XXXVI.

9. Based on interviews of Merwin conducted by himself and by David Elliott, Scigaj makes the case that Merwin, who, like Snyder, has direct and sustained experience with meditative practice, presents as a primary goal of "his best poems" the possibility of "evok[ing] the Zen moment of preverbal suchness, the experience of joyous participation in a world of things with no names" (30). See David L. Elliott, "An Interview with W. S. Merwin," *Contemporary Literature* 39 (spring 1988): 1–25.

10. Scigaj's choice of the French term, while certainly motivated by the potential of its specific meanings, also represents a humorous, if serious, repartee to the devotees of *différance*.

11. Commenting on "Rural Reflections" in 1964, Rich notes that the poem exhibits "an awareness . . . that experience is always greater and more unclassifiable than we give it credit for being" ("Poetry and Experience," 89).

WORKS CITED

Ammons, A. R. *Corsons Inlet: A Book of Poems*. Ithaca: Cornell University Press, 1965.

Aristotle. *On Rhetoric: A Theory of Civic Discourse*. Translated by George A. Kennedy. New York: Oxford University Press, 1991.

Bakhtin, M. M. *The Dialogic Imagination*. Edited by Michael Holquist. Translated by Caryl Emerson and Michael Holquist. Austin: University of Texas Press, 1981.

Bevis, William. *Mind of Winter: Wallace Stevens, Meditation, and Literature*. Pittsburgh: University of Pittsburgh Press, 1988.

Bly, Robert. *News of the Universe: Poems of Twofold Consciousness*. San Francisco: Sierra Club Books, 1980.

Booth, Wayne C. *Modern Dogma and the Rhetoric of Assent*. Chicago: University of Chicago Press, 1974.

Borrelli, Peter. "The River." In *Poems from the Amicus Journal*, 11. Washington, D.C.: Island Press, 1988.

Bramwell, Anna. *Ecology in the Twentieth Century: A History*. New Haven: Yale University Press, 1989.

Buell, Lawrence. *The Environmental Imagination: Thoreau, Nature Writing, and the Formation of American Culture*. Cambridge: Belknap Press-Harvard University Press, 1995.

Burckhardt, Titus. *Art of Islam: Language and Meaning*. N.p.: World of Islam Festival Publishing Co., 1976.

Burke, Kenneth. *A Grammar of Motives*. Berkeley: University of California Press, 1945.

———. *Language as Symbolic Action: Essays on Life, Literature, and Method.* Berkeley: University of California Press, 1966.

———. "(Nonsymbolic) Motion/(Symbolic) Action." *Critical Inquiry* 4 (summer 1978): 809–838.

———. *Permanence and Change: An Anatomy of Purpose.* 1954. Reprint, Berkeley: University of California Press, 1984.

———. *A Rhetoric of Motives.* Berkeley: University of California Press, 1950.

———. *The Rhetoric of Religion: Studies in Logology.* Berkeley: University of California Press, 1961.

Callicott, J. Baird. "Hume's *Is/Ought* Dichotomy and the Relation of Ecology to Leopold's Land Ethic." *Environmental Ethics* 4 (1982): 163–174.

Cardenal, Ernesto. *Nicaraguan New Time.* Translated by Armando Morales. London: Journeyman, 1988.

Coletta, W. John. "The Great Web of Being: Ecological and Evolutionary Aesthetics and the Ideology of Biology." Ph.D. diss., University of Oregon, 1989.

Conley, Thomas M. *Rhetoric in the European Tradition.* New York: Longman, 1990.

De Man, Paul. "Criticism and Crisis." In *Blindness and Insight: Essays in the Rhetoric of Contemporary Criticism.* 2d ed. Minneapolis: University of Minnesota Press, 1971.

Devall, Bill, and George Sessions. *Deep Ecology.* Salt Lake City: Peregrine Smith, 1985.

Dunn, Sara, and Alan Scholefield, eds. *Beneath the Wide Wide Heaven: Poetry of the Environment from Antiquity to the Present.* London: Virago Press, 1991.

Ehrenfeld, David. *The Arrogance of Humanism.* New York: Oxford University Press, 1978.

Elder, John. *Imagining the Earth: The Poetry and the Vision of Nature.* Urbana: University of Illinois Press, 1985.

———. *Reading the Mountains of Home.* Cambridge: Harvard University Press, 1998.

Eliot, T. S. *Four Quartets.* 1943. Reprint, New York: Harcourt Brace Jovanovich, 1971.

———. "The Social Function of Poetry." In *On Poetry and Poets.* New York: Farrar, Straus and Cudahy, 1943, 1957.

Emerson, Ralph Waldo. *Selected Essays.* New York: Penguin, 1982.

Fish, Stanley. *Doing What Comes Naturally: Change, Rhetoric, and the Practice of Theory in Literary and Legal Studies.* Durham: Duke University Press, 1989.

Frost, Carol. *Pure.* Evanston: TriQuarterly Books/Northwestern University Press, 1994.

Frost, Robert. "Education by Poetry." In *Selected Prose of Robert Frost,* 33–46. New York: Holt, Rinehart, 1949, 1966.

———. "The Figure a Poem Makes." In *Selected Prose of Robert Frost,* 17–20. New York: Holt, Rinehart, 1949, 1966.

———. *In the Clearing.* New York: Holt, Rinehart, and Winston, 1962.

———. *Mountain Interval.* New York: Henry Holt and Co., 1916.

———. *New Hampshire.* New York: Henry Holt and Co., 1923.

———. *A Witness Tree.* New York: Henry Holt and Co., 1942.

Gage, John. *In the Arresting Eye: The Rhetoric of Imagism.* Baton Rouge: Louisiana State University Press, 1981.

Gifford, Terry. *Green Voices: Understanding Contemporary Nature Poetry.* Manchester: Manchester University Press, 1995.

Griffin, David Ray, ed. *The Reenchantment of Science: Postmodern Proposals.* Albany: State University of New York Press, 1988.

Heaney, Seamus. *Wintering Out.* London: Faber and Faber, 1972.

Hogan, Linda. *The Book of Medicines.* Minneapolis: Coffee House Press, 1993.

Hume, David. *A Treatise of Human Nature.* Oxford: Clarendon Press, 1960.

Iser, Wolfgang. "The Play of the Text." In *Prospecting: From Reader Response to Literary Anthropology,* 249–261. Baltimore: Johns Hopkins University Press, 1989.

———. "Representation: A Performative Act." In *Prospecting: From Reader Response to Literary Anthropology,* 236–248. Baltimore: Johns Hopkins University Press, 1989.

Jameson, Frederic. *The Prison-House of Language: A Critical Account of Structuralism and Russian Formalism.* Princeton: Princeton University Press, 1972.

Jarman, Mark. "Chimney Swifts." *Crazyhorse* 41 (winter 1991): 70.

Kunitz, Stanley. *Next-to-Last Things: New Poems and Essays.* Boston: Atlantic Monthly Press, 1985.

Lawrence, D. H. *Last Poems.* New York: Viking Press, 1933.

Leopold, Aldo. *A Sand County Almanac.* New York: Oxford University Press, 1949; New York: Ballantine, 1991.

Manes, Christopher. "Nature and Silence." *Environmental Ethics* 14 (1992): 339–350.

Merchant, Carolyn. *Radical Ecology: The Search for a Livable World.* New York: Routledge, 1992.

Merrill, Christopher, ed. *The Forgotten Language: Contemporary Poets and Nature.* Salt Lake City: Peregrine Smith, 1991.

Moore, George Edward. *Principia Ethica.* Cambridge: Cambridge University Press, 1903.

Murphy, Patrick. "Prolegomenon for an Ecofeminist Dialogics." In *Feminism, Bakhtin, and the Dialogic,* edited by Dale Bauer and Susan Jaret McKinstry, 39–56. Albany: State University of New York Press, 1991.

Nietzsche, Friedrich. *On the Genealogy of Morals.* Translated by Walter Kaufmann and R. J. Hollingdale. New York: Vintage/Random House, 1969.

Oelschlaeger, Max. *The Idea of Wilderness: From Prehistory to the Age of Ecology.* New Haven: Yale University Press, 1991.

———. "Wilderness, Civilization, and Language." In *The Wilderness Condition: Essays on Environment and Civilization,* 271–308. San Francisco: Sierra Club Books, 1992.

Pack, Robert. *Fathering the Map.* Chicago: University of Chicago Press, 1993.

Pack, Robert, and Jay Parini, eds. *Poems for a Small Planet: Contemporary American Nature Poetry.* Hanover, N.H.: Middlebury College Press–University Press of New England, 1993.

Penley, Constance, and Andrew Ross. "Cyborgs at Large: Interview with Donna Haraway." In *Technoculture,* 1–20. Minneapolis: University of Minnesota Press, 1991.

Plato. *Gorgias.* Translated by Terence Irwin. Oxford: Clarendon Press, 1979.

———. *Phaedrus.* Translated by R. Hackforth. Cambridge: Cambridge University Press, 1952.

———. *Protagoras*. Translated by B. Jowett. Revised by Martin Ostwald. Edited by Gregory Vlastos. New York: Liberal Arts Press, 1956.

———. *Republic*. Translated by Francis MacDonald Cornford. New York: Oxford University Press, 1945.

Pols, Edward. *Radical Knowing: Direct Knowing in Science and Philosophy*. Ithaca: Cornell University Press, 1992.

Pope, Alexander. *Selected Poetry and Prose*. New York: Rinehart, 1951.

Putman, R. J., and S. D. Wratten. *Principles of Ecology*. Berkeley: University of California Press, 1984.

Regan, Tom. "On the Connection between Environmental Science and Environmental Ethics." *Environmental Ethics* 2 (1980): 363–366.

Rich, Adrienne. "Poetry and Experience: Statement at a Poetry Reading." In *Adrienne Rich's Poetry*, 89. New York: Norton, 1975.

———. *Snapshots of a Daughter-in-Law*. New York: Harper & Row, 1963.

Rolston, Holmes, III. "Is There an Ecological Ethic?" *Ethics* 85 (1975): 93–109.

Roorda, Randall. "KB in Green: Ecology, Critical Theory, and Kenneth Burke." *ISLE* 4:2 (fall 1997): 39–52.

Rorty, Richard. "Cosmopolitanism without Emancipation: A Response to Jean-François Lyotard." In *Objectivity, Relativism, and Truth: Philosophical Papers*. Vol. 1. Cambridge: Cambridge University Press, 1991.

Rotella, Guy. *Reading and Writing Nature: The Poetry of Robert Frost, Wallace Stevens, Marianne Moore, and Elizabeth Bishop*. Boston: Northeastern University Press, 1991.

Russell, Norman H. "The Message of the Rain." In *Poetry from the Amicus Journal*, 59. Palo Alto, CA: Tioga Publishing Co., 1990.

Sadoff, Ira. "In the Bog Behind My House." *The Southern Review* 26 (spring 1990): 326.

Sandilands, Catriona. "From Natural Identity to Radical Democracy." *Environmental Ethics* 17 (1995): 75–91.

Scigaj, Leonard M. *Sustainable Poetry: Four American Ecopoets*. Lexington: The University Press of Kentucky, 1999.

Snyder, Gary. *Axe Handles*. San Francisco: North Point Press, 1983.

———. *The Practice of the Wild*. New York: North Point Press, 1990.

———. *Turtle Island*. New York: New Directions, 1969.

Spivak, Gayatri Chakravorty. "Can the Subaltern Speak?" In *Marxism and the Interpretation of Culture*, edited by Cary Nelson and Lawrence Grossberg, 271–313. Urbana: University of Illinois Press, 1988.

Stafford, William. *Stories That Could Be True: New and Collected Poems.* New York: Harper & Row Publishers, 1977.

Stevens, Wallace. *The Collected Poems of Wallace Stevens.* New York: Alfred A. Knopf, 1978.

Stewart, J. A. *The Myths of Plato.* London: Macmillan, 1905.

Stone, Pat. "John Seed and the Council of All Beings." *Mother Earth News* (May/June 1989): 58–63.

Suzuki, Daisetz T. "Love of Nature." In *Zen and Japanese Culture.* Princeton: Princeton University Press, 1959.

Taylor, Paul W. *Respect for Nature: A Theory of Environmental Ethics.* Princeton: Princeton University Press, 1986.

Voros, Gyorgyi. *Notations of the Wild: Ecology in the Poetry of Wallace Stevens.* Iowa City: University of Iowa Press, 1997.

Williams, Raymond. *The Country and the City.* New York: Oxford University Press, 1973.

Wilson, E. O. *Biophilia.* Cambridge: Harvard University Press, 1984.

Wordsworth, William. *The Selected Poetry and Prose of Wordsworth.* Edited by Geoffrey Hartman. New York: Meridian–New American Library, 1970.

Worster, Donald. *Nature's Economy: A History of Ecological Ideas.* Cambridge: Cambridge University Press, 1985.

Wright, Charles. *Negative Blue.* New York: Farrar, Straus, and Giroux, 2000.

INDEX